RECONSTRUCTION OF A TRAGEDY

RECONSTRUCTION OF A TRAGEDY

The Beverly Hills Supper Club Fire

SOUTHGATE, KENTUCKY
MAY 28, 1977

Prepared by

RICHARD L. BEST
FIRE ANALYSIS SPECIALIST
FIRE INVESTIGATIONS DEPARTMENT
NATIONAL FIRE PROTECTION ASSOCIATION

In cooperation with
NATIONAL FIRE PREVENTION AND CONTROL ADMINISTRATION
and
NATIONAL BUREAU OF STANDARDS
U. S. DEPARTMENT OF COMMERCE

First published in 1978
Copyright © 2020 by Commonwealth Book Company
All Rights Reserved
Printed in the United States of America
ISBN: 978-1-948986-19-9

This investigation was conducted by NFPA under contract to the National Bureau of Standards and the National Fire Prevention and Control Administration, and was jointly funded by the National Bureau of Standards, the National Fire Prevention and Control Administration, and the National Fire Protection Association.

The facts and conclusions contained in this report (except where otherwise noted) were developed by the National Fire Protection Association, and do not necessarily represent the views of the National Fire Prevention and Control Administration or the National Bureau of Standards.

Table of Contents

Section I	**DETAILS OF THE BUILDING**	1
	The Beverly Hills Supper Club, 1	
	Club Expansion and Renovation, 1	
	Construction Features of the Club, 3	
Section II	**RECONSTRUCTION OF THE FIRE**	15
	Events Prior to the Fire, 15	
	Discovery, Alarm, Evacuation, 17	
	Fire Service and Rescue Operations, 39	
	Victims of the Fire, 49	
	Damage to the Building, 52	
	Survivors' Actions and Reactions, 54	
Section III	**ANALYSIS OF THE FIRE**	57
	Origin, Cause, Development, and Spread, 57	
	Life Safety Code Analysis, 63	
	Human Behavior, 75	
	Conclusions and Findings, 80	
	Recommended Areas for Further Study, 82	
	Notes, 83	
	Bibliography, 83	
Appendix A	**QUESTIONNAIRE FORM**	84
Appendix B	**QUESTIONNAIRE DATA**	87
Appendix C	**RICHARD BRIGHT'S ANALYSIS**	91

The Beverly Hills Supper Club is not necessarily the official title of the facility dealt with in this report. The facility was advertised both as the Beverly Hills Country Club and the Beverly Hills "Showplace of the Nation." This report refers to this facility as the Beverly Hills Supper Club and, more simply, as the Club.

Preface

The National Fire Protection Association (NFPA) Fire Investigations Department, in cooperation with the National Bureau of Standards (NBS) and the National Fire Prevention and Control Administration (NFPCA), investigated the Beverly Hills Supper Club fire in order to document and analyze significant factors responsible for the tragic large loss of life. NFPA was notified of the fire on Sunday morning, May 29, 1977, and dispatched two investigators to the scene that day. A total of five NFPA specialists participated in the two-week, on-site investigation. Following this, data collection and analysis of the fire continued over a five-month period. This report, compiled in October, presents findings from these efforts.

Kentucky's official investigation included personnel from the NBS, the NFPA, the NFPCA, the Kentucky State Police, and the Kentucky State Fire Marshal's Office. Members of the Southgate Fire Department (Southgate, Kentucky) participated in the initial phase of the investigation by searching the debris for victims. The Kentucky State Police were responsible for the overall direction and coordination of the investigation, the collection and identification of all evidence, the security of the site during the investigation, and the release of information. In September 1977, the Commonwealth of Kentucky released its report, "Investigation Report to the Governor, Beverly Hills Supper Club Fire, May 28, 1977."[1]

The quotations used in this NFPA report, unless otherwise noted, are taken from the transcripts compiled by the Kentucky State Police. During transcription, some words were parenthetically added or questioned by transcribers. In addition, NFPA also added comments for clarification of the quoted material. All added words and comments have been enclosed in parentheses. The real names of the individuals referred to in the transcripts have been changed in all but a few instances; these changes are also referred to in parentheses.

In addition to the wealth of transcribed information the Kentucky State Police mailed a twenty-two-item survey questionnaire, developed with the assistance of the NFPA, to several hundred individuals. Its purpose was to collect information about the occurrences on the night of the fire in a systematic manner to permit statistical analysis of the data and an objective interpretation of the results. A multiple-choice format was chosen, although open-ended questions were used when appropriate. The questionnaire and a summary of the questionnaire responses are included in Appendices A and B of this report. Data from the questionnaires has also been incorporated into this report.

The figures of the Beverly Hills Supper Club included in this report are as accurate as possible, and are compiled from a careful analysis of building plans, on-site examination, actual dimensions (when available), and patron and employee statements. However, the figures may contain minor inaccuracies in some areas due to: (1) the nearly complete destruction of portions of the Club by the fire, and (2) the fact that a complete set of "as-built" plans of the Club apparently does not exist. Some areas of the building were not shown on the existing building plans; in some instances, on-site examination revealed areas that were not constructed as shown on building plans. There was conflicting evidence concerning the swing of the double doors at the northeast corner of the Cabaret Room. Since this was an important detail in the means of egress analysis, two possible arrangements are presented in this report. (See page 64.)

Although the Beverly Hills Supper Club did not have a true north-south, east-west orientation, such an orientation has been assumed for ease of description.

Acknowledgments

The cooperation and assistance of the Kentucky State Police and the Kentucky State Fire Marshal's Office is greatly appreciated by the NFPA. Although the individuals involved during the investigation are too numerous to acknowledge individually, the monumental task of conducting an investigation of this magnitude could not possibly have been accomplished by any one agency and without the professional dedication of the following individuals:

Lewis Babb, Jr., Lieutenant Colonel, Director of the Division of Criminal Investigations, Kentucky State Police
Kenneth E. Brandenburgh, Commissioner, Kentucky State Police
Richard G. Bright, Senior Research Engineer, Center for Fire Research, National Bureau of Standards.
Gerard D'Errico, Visual Presentations, Inc. of Maynard, Massachusetts
Thomas A. Klem, National Fire Data Center, National Fire Prevention and Control Administration.
Dr. Ovid Lewis, Professor of Law, Northern Kentucky University
Richard Riesenberg, Fire Chief, Southgate Fire Department
Warren Southworth, Kentucky State Fire Marshal

The assistance of NFPA personnel is also gratefully acknowledged:

James Lathrop, Fire Analysis Specialist
John Sharry, *Life Safety Code* Specialist
Joseph Ross, Electrical Specialist
Joseph Swartz, Research Division Director

Others who aided in the production of the original manuscript were: supervision and coordination of manuscript preparation by Gail A. Fournier (NFPA Systems Development Secretary); technical review by Dr. John L. Bryan (Professor and Chairman, Department of Fire Protection Engineering, University of Maryland) and A. Elwood Willey (Director, Fire Information and Systems Division, NFPA); and technical assistance by Dr. Geoffrey N. Berlin (Principal Operations Research Analyst, NFPA).

Excerpts from *An Analysis of the Development and Spread of Fire from the Room of Fire Origin (Zebra Room) to the Cabaret Room* by Richard G. Bright[2] have been utilized in various sections of this report; Mr. Bright's complete analysis appears in Appendix C.

Special credit is given to the Kentucky State Police for their unusual and exceptional level of effort towards gathering as much information as they did about the events of the fire, and their willingness to share that information with other agencies analyzing the Beverly Hills Supper Club tragedy. Much of the information in this report is based on transcripts of interviews that were conducted by the Kentucky State Police and the Kentucky State Police arson investigators.

Summary

On Saturday, May 28, 1977, a disastrous fire occurred at the Beverly Hills Supper Club in Southgate, Kentucky, that claimed the lives of 164 patrons and employees and injured some seventy others. This fire was the worst multiple-death building fire in the United States since the Cocoanut Grove night club burned in Boston on November 28, 1942, taking 492 lives.

The Beverly Hills Supper Club — classified as a place of assembly — was a sprawling, mostly one-story restaurant and night club that was over an acre in area. A small part of the building was two-story, and there was a basement under approximately half of the complex. The original two-story portion was constructed in 1937; additions were added at various times, with a major rebuilding of the Club following a fire in 1970.

The building was basically of unprotected, noncombustible-type construction, and did not have automatic sprinkler protection, a fire detection system, or an alarm system. The Club was populated by about 2,400 to 2,800 people on the night of the fire, with approximately 1,200 to 1,300 people attending a show in a large showroom, the Cabaret Room, which featured well-known entertainers.

A fire originating in a small, unoccupied function room on the opposite end of the Club burned for a considerable time before discovery. The probable cause was determined to be electrical in nature, with the ignition of combustible material in a concealed space. When the fire was discovered, the Beverly Hills Supper Club staff unsuccessfully attempted to fight the fire before notifying the fire department or alerting occupants in the building to evacuate. Most of the patrons were evacuated with the assistance of employees. However, when the Cabaret Room occupants were made aware of the fire emergency, they did not have adequate time nor sufficient egress capacity to escape. Many were overcome by fire gases and smoke. Nearly all of the 164 fatalities were occupants of the Cabaret Room.

Following the fire an examination and analysis of the facts revealed many facility and operational deviations from national consensus fire codes and standards, particularly NFPA 101, *Code for Safety to Life from Fire in Buildings and Structures* (the NFPA *Life Safety Code*). The major contributing factors to the large loss of life in this fire include:

• The fire in the Zebra Room developed for a considerable time, and discovery was delayed. The presence of concealed combustible ceiling tile and wood materials used for supports provided a fuel supply for continued spread of the fire through the original and other concealed spaces. Following discovery, this fire posed a severe threat to occupants.

• The Beverly Hills Supper Club staff attempted to extinguish the fire before notifying occupants to evacuate from the building, and prior to calling the fire department. There was no evacuation plan establishing fire emergency procedures for the Beverly Hills Supper Club, and employees were not schooled or drilled in duties they were to perform in case of fire.

- The number of people in the Cabaret Room exceeded almost triple the number of occupants that the room could safely accommodate. Also, the number of occupants in the Beverly Hills Supper Club (total building) on the night of the fire exceeded almost double the number of people that the building could safely accommodate.

- The capacity of the means of egress for the Club — and especially for the Cabaret Room — was not adequate for the occupant load, based on square feet per occupant, or for the actual number of occupants that were in the building at the time of the fire.

- The interior finish in the main north-south corridor exceeded the flame spread allowed for places of assembly in the NFPA *Life Safety Code,* and contributed to the rapid spread of fire from the Zebra Room to the Cabaret Room.

- The Beverly Hills Supper Club was not provided with automatic sprinkler protection as required by the NFPA *Life Safety Code* and the *National Building Code,* in effect at the time of the fire.

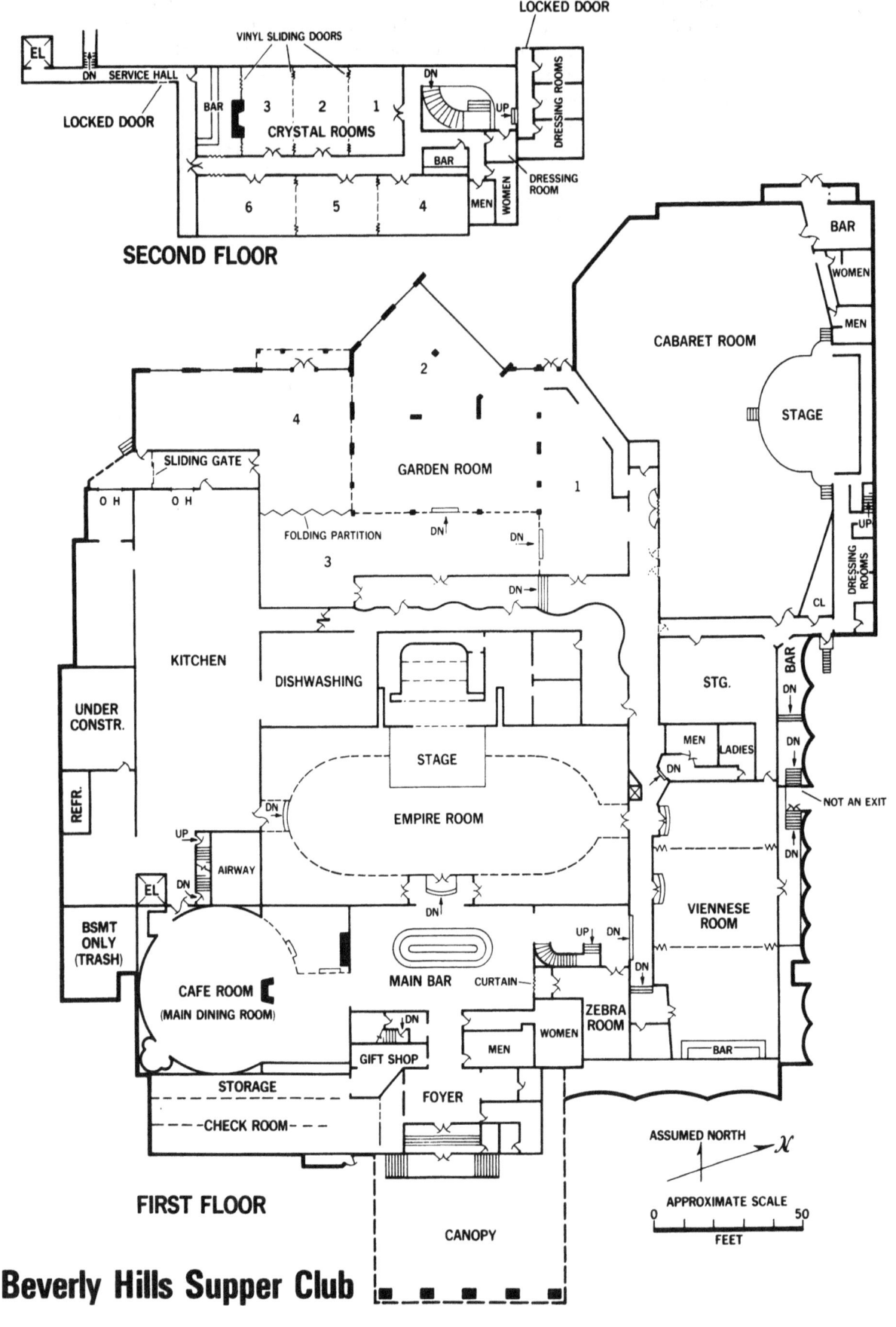

The Beverly Hills Supper Club Fire

Section I

DETAILS OF THE BUILDING

THE BEVERLY HILLS SUPPER CLUB

Billed as "The Showplace of the Nation," the Beverly Hills Supper Club was located in Southgate, Kentucky, in the Greater Cincinnati area. Well-known entertainers performed nightly in the Cabaret Room. Banquets, dinner dances, balls, business meetings, fashion shows, and receptions were regularly held in the Club's numerous dining and party rooms. Complete weddings could even be performed at the Club, including a wedding service in the chapel at the rear of the Club, photographs in the formal garden, and a reception and dinner in one of the dining rooms.

The Beverly Hills Supper Club advertised eighteen rooms that offered accommodations for twenty to 1,000 persons. The building actually contained five main dining rooms in addition to the large Cabaret Room, a small function room known as the Zebra Room, and the *Directoire* Lounge, which will be referred to as the main bar. Three of the large dining rooms could be subdivided into smaller rooms by the use of folding partitions, thereby forming eighteen separate dining areas in addition to the main bar. The main dining room, which was also referred to as the Cafe dining room, was advertised as the *Cafe Frontenac*. A beautiful hallway lined with mirrors, appropriately called the Hallway of the Mirrors, had an open, curved stairway known as the Cinderella Stairway, which was lavishly decorated.

The Club operated six days a week, Tuesday through Sunday. Shows in the Cabaret Room started at 8:30 p.m. and 10:30 p.m. on Tuesday through Thursday; at 8:30 p.m. and 11:30 p.m. on Friday and Saturday; and at 7:30 p.m. and 10:30 p.m. on Sunday.

Patrons had the options of eating dinner before the show, or having dinner following the show. Some parties would eat without attending the show, and others would attend the show without dining at the Club. All show patrons and dining room patrons were handled by reservation only. A "cubbyhole" located on one side of the front bar outside the Zebra Room was the location where the reservationist sat to take telephone reservations. This area was concealed from the bar by a curtain hung over the opening. Patrons who had reservations would normally be directed to the front bar to wait for a table. They would then be directed to one of the rooms and would be seated by a hostess.

CLUB EXPANSION AND RENOVATION

The original, two-story Beverly Hills Supper Club was constructed in 1937 and was approximately 56 feet by 164 feet. The building was purchased by the 4-R Corporation in 1969, and a substantial remodeling of the building was undertaken at that time. Before the remodeling was completed, a fire occurred in the structure on June 21, 1970, that caused damage to a large area of the building presently identified as the Empire Room and adjoining areas. Photographs of the 1970 fire indicate that the fire damaged a large area of the Club, with roof collapse over an extensive area.

Following the fire, a permit to rebuild was issued by the Southgate building inspector in December 1970, and the Club was rebuilt. The Beverly Hills Supper Club reopened for business in 1971.

In July 1974, a building permit was issued by the city of Southgate for the Cabaret Room expansion. Addi-

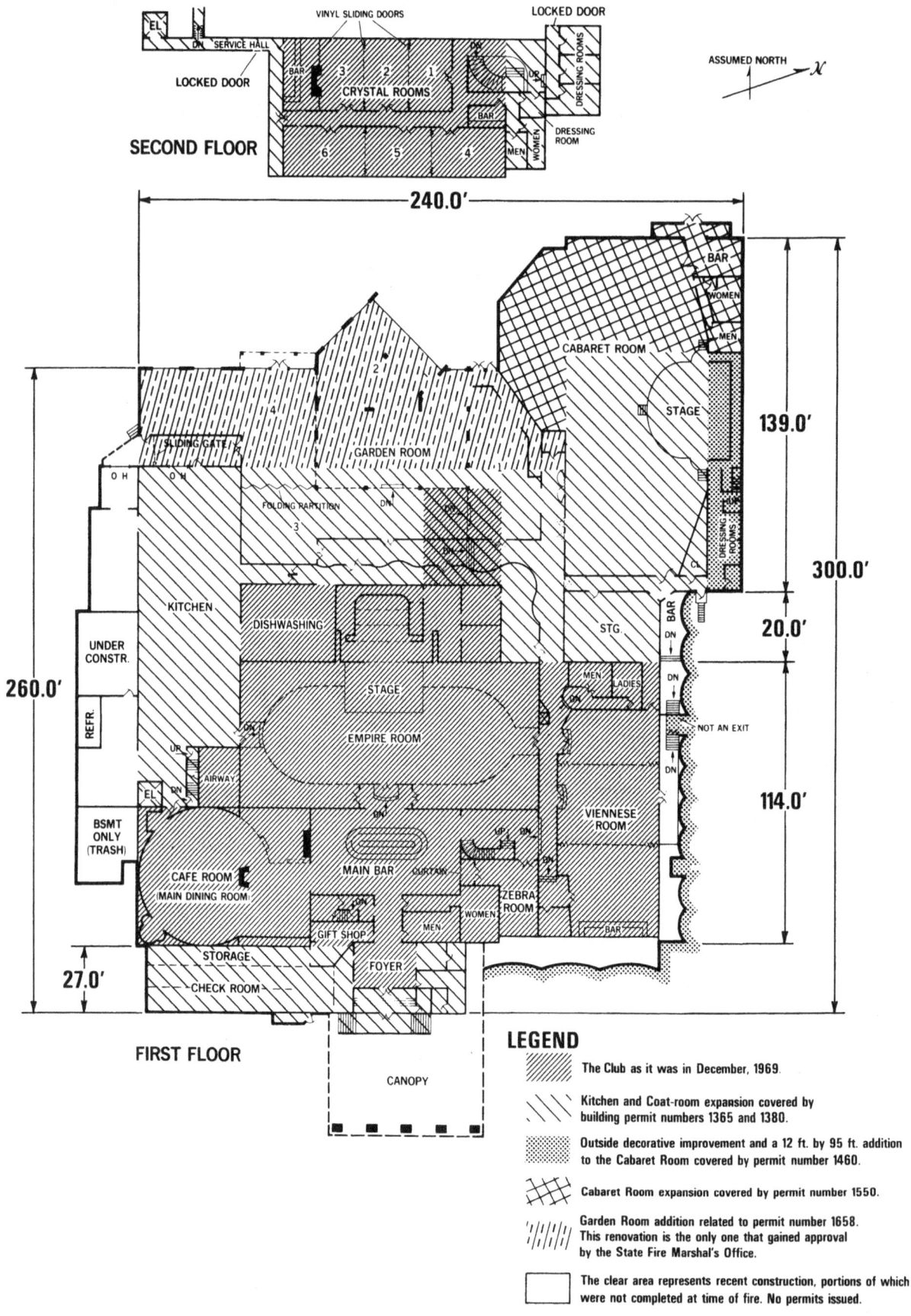

Figure 1.

Table 1.1 The Standards of Safety for The Commonwealth of Kentucky

	Standard*	Effective date
1. 1963 SS	*National Building Code (NBC)*, 1955 Ed., with 1957 and 1963 amendments; *National Electrical Code (NEC)*, 1962 Ed.	March 15, 1963
2. 1972 SS	*NBC*, 1967 Ed.; *National Fire Codes (NFC)*, Vols. 1 to 10, 1970-71 Ed.; *NEC*, 1968 Ed.	January 14, 1972
3. 1973 SS	*NBC*, 1967 Ed.; *NFC*, Vols. 1 to 10, 1972-73 Ed.; *NEC*, 1971 Ed.	November 7, 1973
4. 1974 SS	*NBC*, 1967 Ed.; *NFC*, Vols. 1 to 10, 1973-74 Ed.; *NEC*, 1971 Ed.	November 20, 1974
5. 1977 SS	*NBC*, 1976 Ed.; *NFC*, Vols. 1 to 16, 1976 Ed.; *NEC*, 1975 Ed.	April 6, 1977

*The NFPA *National Fire Codes* for various years contain the following editions of NFPA 101, *Code for Safety to Life from Fire in Buildings and Structures* (the *Life Safety Code*): 1970-71 *National Fire Codes*, 1967 Ed. of the *Life Safety Code*; 1972-73 *National Fire Codes*, 1970 Ed. of the *Life Safety Code*; 1973-74 and 1976 *National Fire Codes*, 1973 Ed. of the *Life Safety Code*.

tional building permits were issued by the city of Southgate for additions and remodeling, although other additions and remodeling were completed without building permits. (See Figure 1.)

The standards of safety of the Commonwealth of Kentucky, in effect from the time of the 1970 substantial remodeling until May 28, 1977, are outlined in Table 1.1. In addition to these codes, cities may adopt local ordinances that are effective to the extent that they are at least as stringent as the state standards of safety.[3] The city of Southgate did adopt a building code in 1947 that dealt with areas covered by the standards of safety and did adopt local ordinances. The pertinent sequence of enactments by the city is as follows:

• February 1942: Southgate adopted the 1941 Standards of Safety (Ord. No. 42-[5]).

• October 2, 1946: The 1946 Standards of Safety were adopted (Ord. No. 72-[5]).

• July 2, 1947: The Building Code was adopted (Ord. No. 75-[5]).

• January 19, 1949: Ord. No. 72-(5) was amended and the 1948 Standards of Safety adopted (Ord. No. 87-[5]).

• May 15, 1956: Ord. No. 87-(5) was repealed and Ord. No. 72-(5) was amended, and the 1955 Standards of Safety were adopted (Ord. No. 139-[5]).

• October 15, 1958: The Building Code (Ord. No. 75-[5]) was amended (Ord. No. 159-[5]).

• February 5, 1964: Ord. No. 139-(5) was repealed and the 1963 Standards of Safety adopted (Ord. No. 217-[5]).*

CONSTRUCTION FEATURES OF THE CLUB

The Beverly Hills Supper Club was an irregularly-shaped building approximately 240 feet by 260 feet, or about 65,500 square feet. Except for a basement area under approximately one-half of the building (the front portion, or south side) and a small second-floor area over the main bar at the south side of the building, the building was essentially one-story. (See Figures 2 and 3.)

Basically, construction of the building was unprotected noncombustible. However, the nearly complete destruction of the building made it extremely difficult to determine construction details for all areas. In addition, the fire-resistance rating of the roof-ceiling and floor-ceiling assemblies was not determined, but many areas, such as the basement, had no suspended ceilings and no protection of the exposed steel columns and beams. Many areas of the complex had recessed, high-hat, and bathroom light fixtures that penetrated the suspended ceilings in numerous places.

*See "Assessment of Compliance with Applicable Law," *Investigative Report To The Governor — Beverly Hills Supper Club Fire*, for an assessment of the role of Southgate standards of safety.

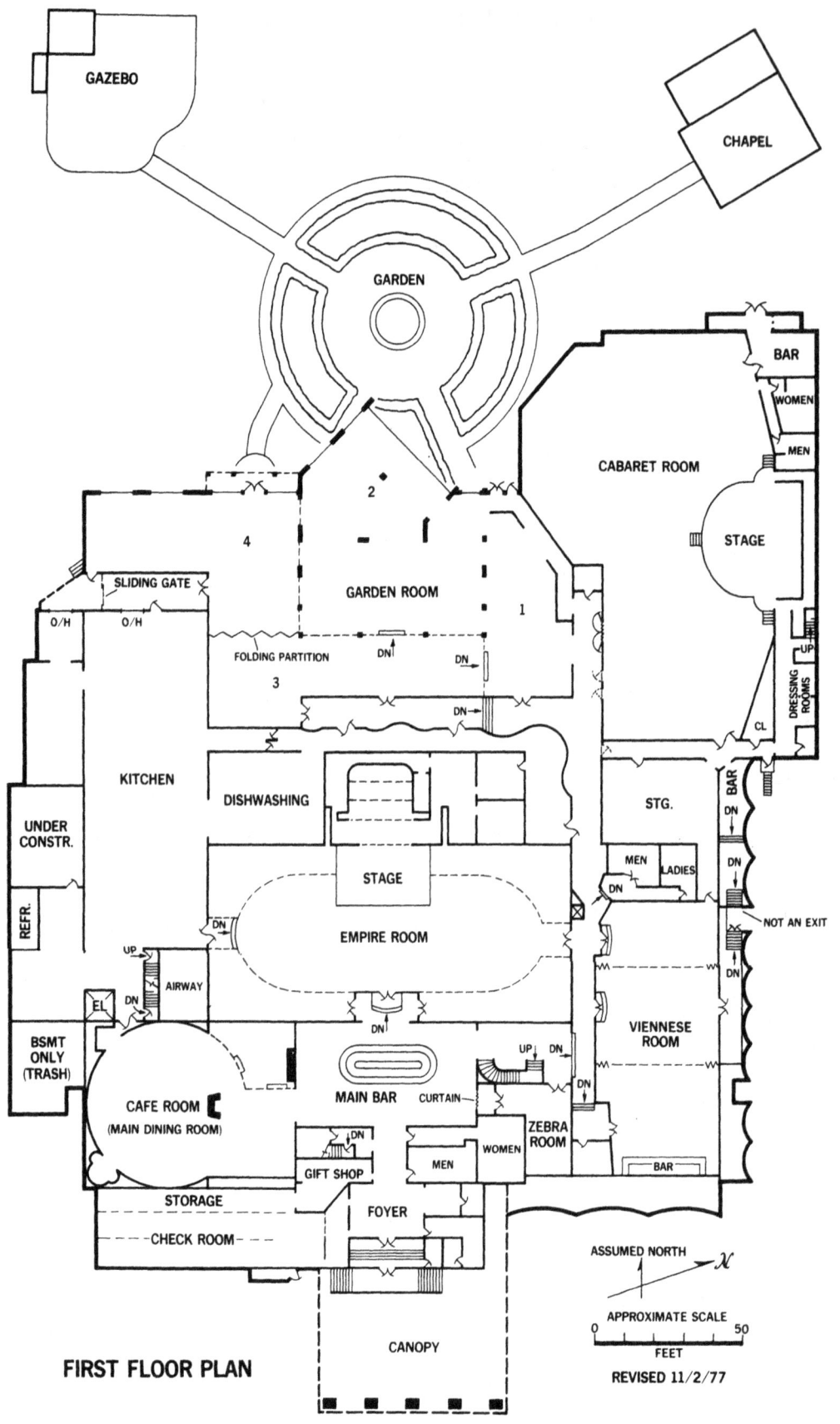

Figure 2.

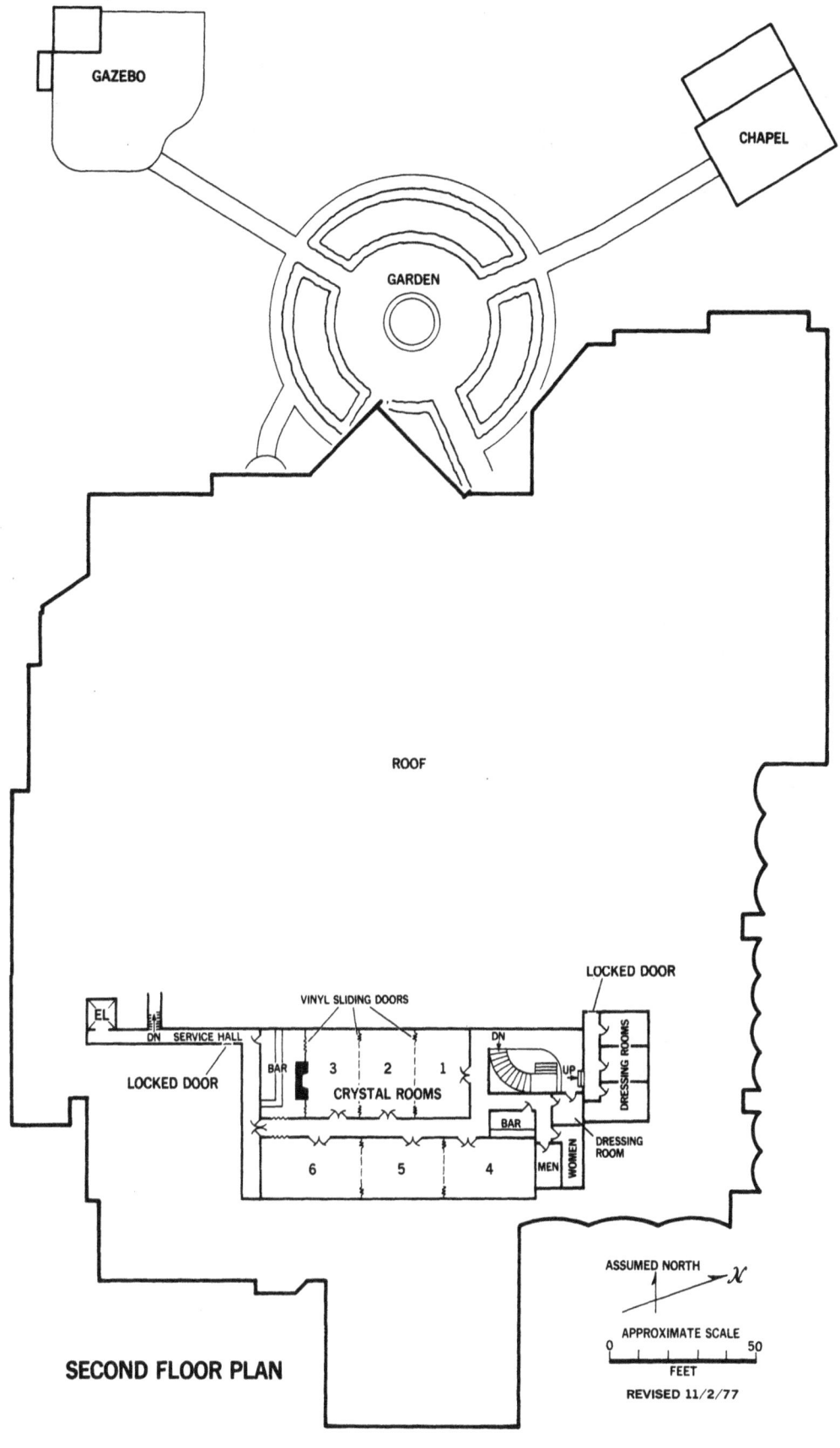

Figure 3.

RECONSTRUCTION OF A TRAGEDY

A before-the-fire view of the front entrance to the Beverly Hills Supper Club, as seen from the driveway. Note the windowless facade of the Club.

The two-story-and-basement section of the building was the oldest part of the Club. It was constructed of steel column and beam framing. Outside walls were brick and concrete block, with poured concrete basement walls; first and second floors were poured concrete on steel mesh on steel bar joists; and the basement floor was poured concrete. The roof construction was a built-up type on steel deck on steel bar joists. There were suspended ceilings through all areas of the first and second floors consisting of plaster on metal lath, 12-inch-by-12-inch and 2-foot-by-4-foot suspended ceiling tiles. Many areas had suspended ceilings that were installed below the original plaster on metal lath ceilings.

The 1970 expansion and renovation and other expansion projects consisted of a new kitchen, the Garden Rooms, the Cabaret Room, and a small storage room. All additions except the kitchen and coatroom were one-story, with concrete block and brick walls. A glassed-in area of 60 feet long was

A before-the-fire view of the cafe dining room, looking from the northeast to the southwest corner of the room. (Credit: Kentucky State Police)

located at the rear of the Garden Rooms. Floors were concrete, and roofs were a built-up roof cover on steel deck on steel bar joists.

The kitchen consisted of one story and a basement, and was of similar construction to other additions north of the two-story original building. Walls were concrete block and poured concrete. The first floor construction was poured concrete on steel deck on 12-inch steel trusses. A newly constructed addition to the kitchen on the west side of the complex had masonry walls with a wood-joisted floor.

The coatroom addition, 27 feet by 82 feet, was at the southwest corner of the Club, and was one-story with a garage-like storage area underneath. The walls of the storage area were concrete block. The first-floor level of the coatroom was wood-frame construction, with wood joist floor supports, interior wood framing, and aluminum siding on the west outside wall.

Wood framing was used in many areas for stage construction and interior wall partitions. The partitions separating the bar and toilet areas from the Cabaret Room were constructed with wood studding. The second floor over the Zebra Room was constructed with interior wood framing and plywood flooring, and a wood roof. Many of these small areas appeared to be ordinary construction (concrete block or brick exterior bearing walls, with floors and interior framing wholly or partly of wood).

There were no intermediate roof supports in any of the various rooms at the Beverly Hills Supper Club, with the possible exception of the Garden Rooms. Those intermediate supports are believed to be the walls of older sections that were left in place when the Garden Rooms were expanded. The roof spans in the various showrooms and other rooms extended from wall to wall. The piecemeal construction of the Club, with rooms and groups of rooms being added at different times, resulted in a structure with no common ceiling space. In other words, the walls between rooms, in most cases,* were outside walls at one time. They were extended to the roof or above the roof with no opening between rooms above the suspended ceilings. Where additions were made to existing buildings, window openings were not sealed with a masonry material to provide some degree of fire cutoff between rooms, and no attempt was made to protect door openings or to provide smoke or fire partitions. Likewise, the boiler room and kitchen were not separated from other parts of the building with enclosures having a fire-resistance rating and with openings protected by self-closing or automatic-closing fire-rated assemblies.

---

*For example, the wall between the Zebra Room and the Viennese Rooms, or at the second floor between the Crystal Rooms and the toilet area over the Zebra Room.

Openings Between Floors

The main, curved stairway between the first and second floors was of metal construction. A small decorative pool was located under the stairway. The stairs were open from the first floor to the second floor, with no stairway enclosure and no doors at openings to the stairway from the first floor main bar or Viennese Rooms, or from the corridor on the second floor.

The stairway on the west side of the complex from the second floor to the kitchen was 44 inches wide and was concrete-block-enclosed. Three-foot-wide metal doors opened into the stair enclosure, with the door at the bottom of the stairs opening against the direction of travel of people coming down the stairs. The stair treads and risers were of wood construction.

Zebra Room Construction

The Zebra Room was a small function room on the first floor located on the south side of the building be-

The open, curved stairway — The Cinderella Stairway — leading to the second floor Crystal Rooms. Note the decorative fountain below the stairway, and the entrance to the Zebra Room to the rear of the first floor landing. (Credit: Kentucky State Police)

RECONSTRUCTION OF A TRAGEDY

tween the Viennese Rooms and the main bar. The room was *L*-shaped, with the main area being 15 feet by 30 feet. The smaller alcove was 8 feet 9 inches, by 9 feet. (See Figure 4.) The basement was under the Zebra Room. Toilets were above on the second floor.

The south and east walls of the 15-foot-by-30-foot rectangular area of the Zebra Room were brick. The east wall was covered with ¾-inch-by-4-inch furring boards covered with gypsum board. Hardboard paneling on wood furring strips covered the plaster board. The finish material on the south wall was not determined, except that a factory-built metal fireplace was located in the outside window and was vented a few feet up the outside wall (between the exterior wall and the screen wall) with a metal stack. The fireplace contained ceramic logs and was gas-fired, but reportedly was not used.

The west wall of the Zebra Room was nonloadbearing, 2-by-6 wood stud from the floor to a wide-flange steel beam at the second floor level, and was brick wall above the beam. The wooden studding was covered with plaster on gypsum board, and the plaster was covered with hardboard panel on wood furring.

The north Zebra Room wall was wood stud covered with plaster on metal lath on both sides. The inside wall was similar to other walls previously described, with the plaster covered with wood furring and hardboard paneling. All sides of the small Zebra Room alcove were nearly totally destroyed by the fire, but were determined to be wood stud construction. Reportedly, double doors were located on the west wall opening from the main bar.

The ceiling in the Zebra Room was double suspended, with a combustible fiberboard tile adhered to the plaster ceiling that was nearest to the steel bar joist of the floor above. The Zebra Room floor was poured concrete on steel bar joist. (See Figure 5.)

Interior Finish

The Beverly Hills Supper Club was decorated throughout the function facilities and showrooms with huge chandeliers, wood and hardboard paneling, carpeting, and drapes, all of which contributed to the aura of an elegant showplace. The north wall of the hallway outside the Zebra Room had a wood studded wall covered with wood paneling, plywood, and mirrors that were spaced away from the brick wall. The ceiling in this corridor was a mineral-type acoustical tile. The floor was carpeted with the same carpeting that was used in the Zebra Room. That carpet was identified by the National Bureau of Standards as a low pile height nylon carpet of dense construction, with an unidentified padding.

The main north-south corridor, which went from the small hallway outside the Zebra Room to the Cabaret and Garden Rooms, also had a ceiling of mineral-type acoustical tile. The floor was covered with a carpet which, according to the National Bureau of Standards,[4] was of a woven wool construction with a small amount of acrylic fibers. The underlayment was identified as jute. The walls of this corridor were covered with hardboard paneling applied over wood furring strips. This hardboard paneling was applied on both walls of the corridor for its full length, except for the curvilinear wall at the west cross corridor, which was exposed brick, and another section of the corridor near the Cabaret Room, which was paneled on one side with interior doors placed side-by-side.

Means of Egress

Exits to the outside of the building are shown with a letter designation assigned to each exit. (See Figure 6.) Problems regarding exit marking, exit access, locked exits, and the adequacy of exits are discussed in Section III, "*Life Safety Code* Analysis"; however, for a better understanding of conditions in the Beverly Hills Supper Club at the time of the fire, certain egress features should be understood.

The exit from the east side of the Viennese Rooms (Exit C) led to a concrete platform that was between the original outside wall of the building and a false front (facade) that had been constructed along the east side of the Club. The platform led to steps and to double doors to the outside. The door from the Viennese Rooms was reportedly camouflaged by drapes to look like a window. A waitress gave the following description of the Viennese Rooms exit after the fire: "It was along here somewhere, it was in the Viennese Rooms, because they had these curtains tied up there and they're fake windows, but they did have a sign. I never went out it, but I remember seeing the sign that had 'exit' over it." A piano player in the band in the Viennese Rooms stated that he thought the door to the corridor was the only exit from the room. The operational status of the exit door from the east side of the Viennese Rooms (Exit C) at the time of the fire could not be determined. A chain and padlock was found attached to the panic hardware from one of the double doors after the fire, but the area was too severely damaged to determine if the chain was arranged to prevent the door from opening. One single exit door from the north side of the Club (Exit H) was reported to be locked at the time of the fire. The door was close beside the double doors at Exit G.

In addition to the main, curved stairway from the second floor to the first floor and the service stairway to the kitchen, there were two doors to the roof that

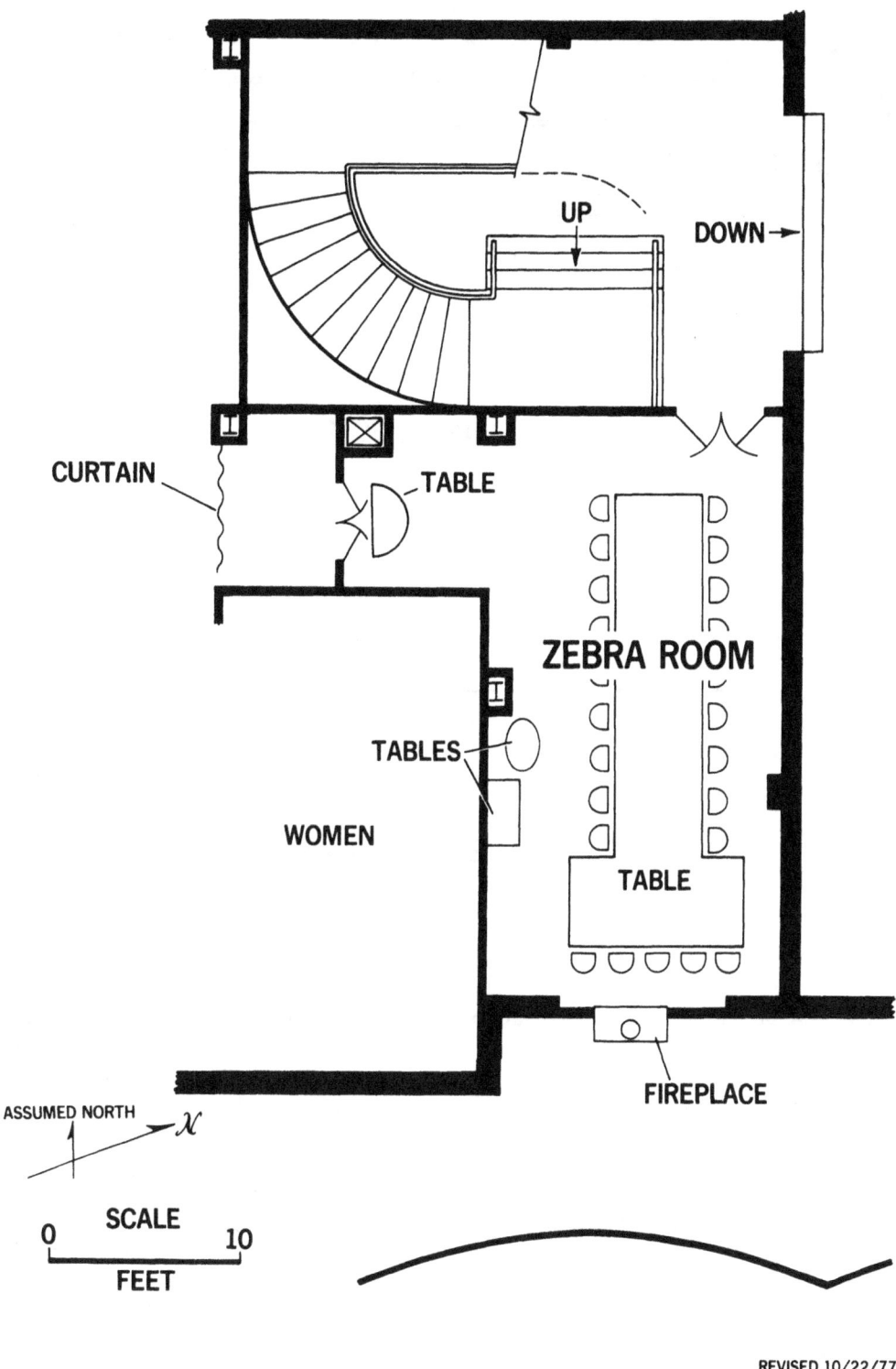

ZEBRA ROOM

Figure 4.

were locked. There was no safe means of egress from the roof, and the doors were not considered exits.

The way to reach an exit was not clearly indicated in all areas of the Beverly Hills Supper Club. There were exit signs in the Cabaret Room indicating the location of the southeast and northeast exits from the room,

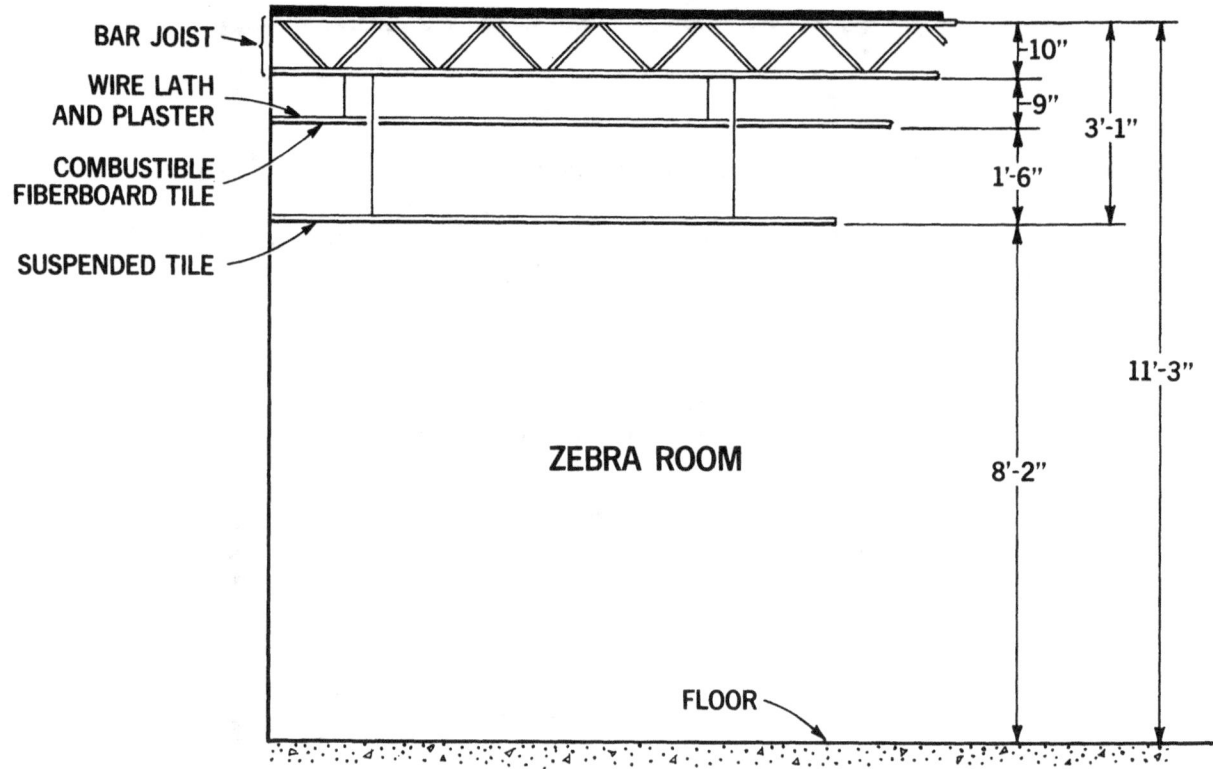

ZEBRA ROOM CEILING SECTION VIEW

Figure 5.

but beyond the double doors there was no indication of the direction to the exit. (See Figure 7.)

The entire east side of the building was built on the edge of a very steep slope that went downward from the Club toward the highway. There was a narrow path along the side of the building from Exits B and C toward the front of the building.

A sliding gate was located in the path of travel from the north end of the kitchen and the west side of the Garden Rooms. West of the gate was a concrete loading dock with narrow, concrete steps to the driveway.

Heating, Ventilating, and Air Conditioning (HVAC)

Sufficient information regarding the heating and air conditioning systems at the Beverly Hills Supper Club was not available following the fire to determine the arrangement and operation of the equipment. The nearly complete destruction of major portions of the building was compounded by a lack of plans of the HVAC and the absence of a plant engineer or maintenance man who knew the system.

An air conditioning service company that had serviced the equipment at the Club was contacted by the State Fire Marshal's Office. The persons who were contacted reportedly were very reluctant to offer information, and would only answer direct questions.

There was air handling equipment in the basement that was apparently original equipment that supplied both hot and cold air to both the first and second floors of the original building. Heat was provided by steam coils, and cold air was from refrigeration coils in the air handling systems. Two main ducts went up a shaftway at the circular stairs. One duct went to the ladies' room, foyer, main bar, and Zebra Room. The other duct supplied the second floor.

As additions to the Club were constructed, rooftop air conditioning/heating units were added to handle the increased load. Approximately eleven rooftop units were found in the remains of the building after the fire. It was reported by an employee that the units controlled individual rooms and areas. There was no distribution system linking the front area of the Club with the rear Garden Rooms and Cabaret Room.

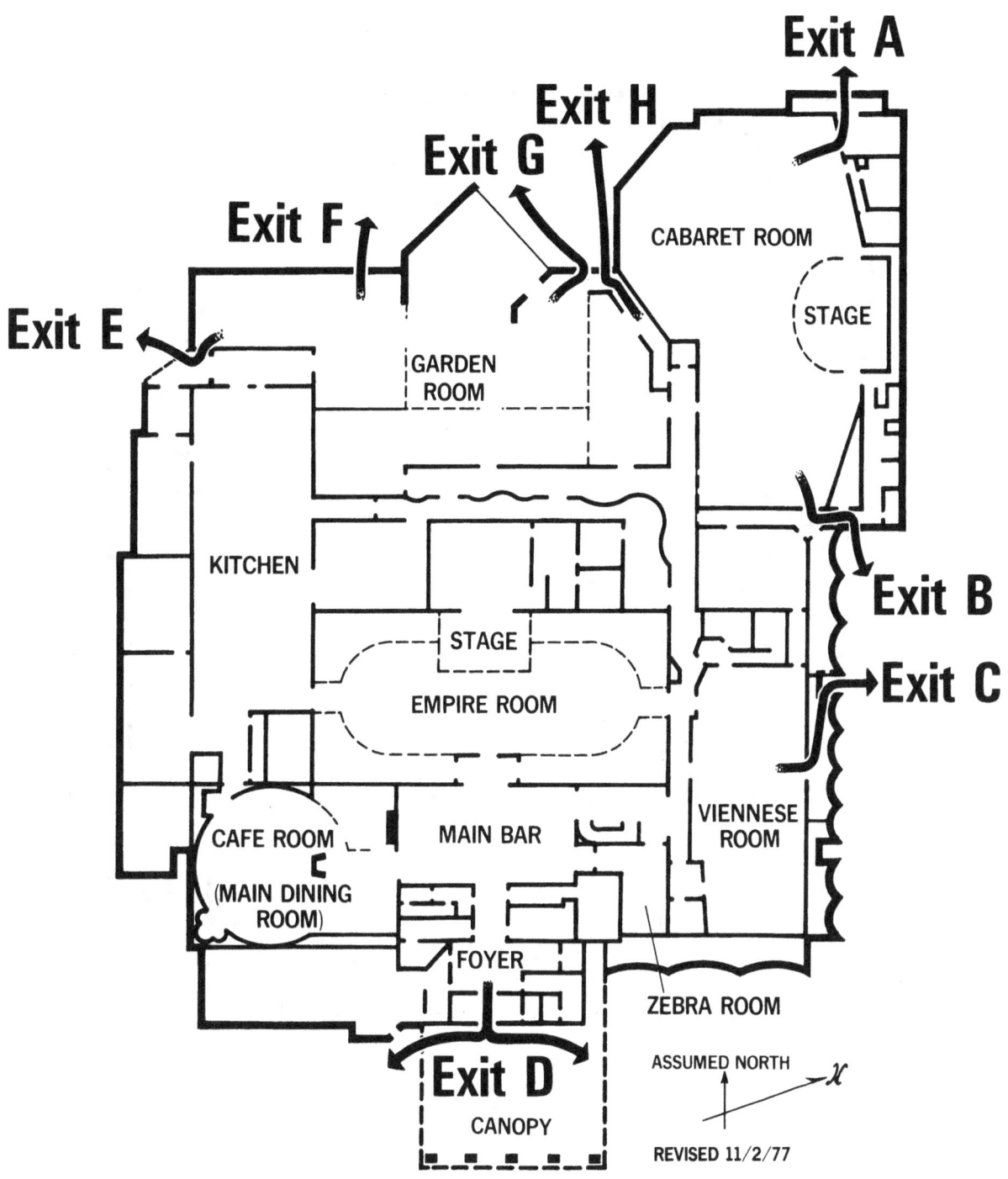

EXIT CODE

Figure 6.

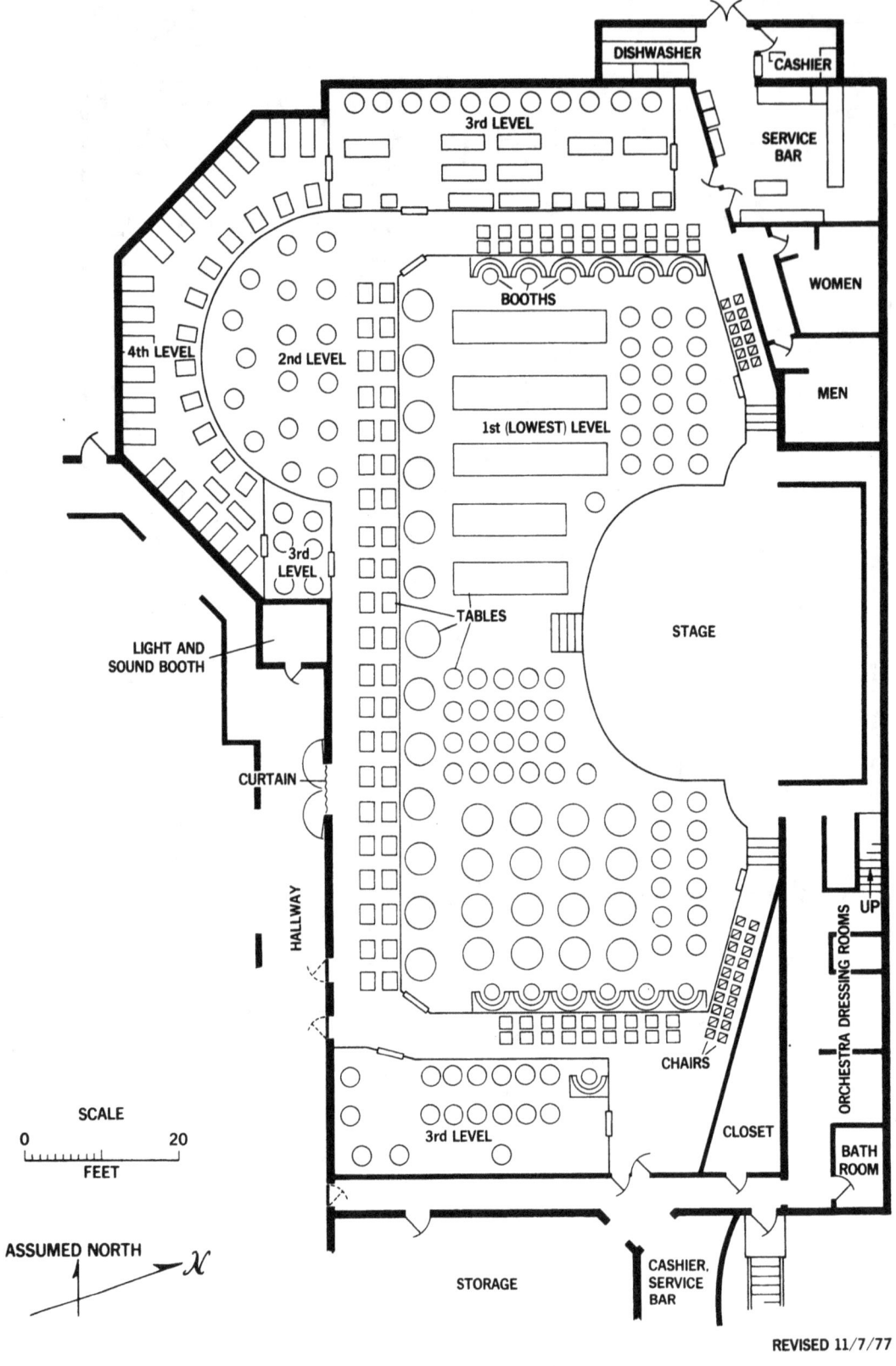

CABARET ROOM

Figure 7.

THE BEVERLY HILLS SUPPER CLUB FIRE

A before-the-fire view of the Cabaret Room, looking from northwest to southeast. The date of the photo is unknown.

Fire Protection

Fire protection at the Beverly Hills Supper Club consisted of portable fire extinguishers. There were no sprinkler or standpipe systems, no fixed protection of the kitchen hoods or deep fat fryers, no alarm system, and no fire or smoke detection systems.

The building was protected by a fully volunteer fire department that was rated Grade 6 by the Insurance Services Office (ISO). The Southgate Volunteer Fire Department operates two engines out of one station located 1.1 miles from the Beverly Hills Supper Club. The Club's location was previously graded Class 8 because of limited water supply, although it is believed that the water supply has since been improved.

Water flow tests of the public and private hydrants in the immediate area of the Beverly Hills Supper Club were made by the Newport Fire Department during a prefire plan drill. Complete static and residual pressure readings were not available to enable a proper evaluation of the gallons per minute (gpm) data developed. It was reported that the hydrant on the south corner of the Club and the hydrant southeast of the Oasis (a dining establishment on the highway below the Club) were fed from an old 4-inch main, and provided a flow of under 250 gpm.

The hydrants immediately east of the Beverly Hills Supper Club and northwest of the Beverly Hills Supper Club driveway on Alexandria Pike apparently were supplied by newer water mains, and provided flows in the range of 1,500 gpm.

The Southgate Volunteer Fire Department has eighty-three dues-paying members. Fifty-five of the members are active fire fighters, including six young people between the ages of 16 and 18 who train with the fire department in anticipation of joining the department when they are old enough.

The department operates from a single fire station. Their equipment consists of a 1974, 1,000-gpm triple combination pumper; a 1964, 750-gpm triple combination pumper; a 1974 utility van referred to as a light rescue; and a 1971 ambulance. The department is dispatched by radio from the Campbell County Police Dispatch Center, as are all Campbell County Fire Departments except fully paid departments. The Southgate Volunteer Fire Department has fifty-four tone alert radio receivers in members' homes. The department has mutual aid arrangements and participates in the Northern Kentucky Move-Up System.*

---

*A tricounty mutual aid agreement whereby during a major fire, fire departments with more than one piece of fire apparatus will move-up under a preplanned schedule.

The Beverly Hills Supper Club Fire

Section II

RECONSTRUCTION OF THE FIRE

EVENTS PRIOR TO THE FIRE

On the evening of May 28, 1977, singer John Davidson was scheduled to appear at the Beverly Hills Supper Club at an 8:30 p.m. show and an 11:30 p.m. show. A dining area hostess stated that:

- Not all parties go to the show. So there's still maybe 3 or 4 party rooms of people and the parties, depending on the room that they're in, can range from maybe 20 people to 500 to 600 people.

Employees reported to work throughout the afternoon. The beverage manager, a bartender, and a cleaning lady had started working in the early afternoon to midafternoon. Waitresses and waiters came in between 4:00 p.m. to 6:00 p.m.

Two parties were scheduled in the upstairs Crystal Rooms; one of the groups was having a fashion show. Models in the fashion show reported to the Club at approximately 6:00 p.m. to eat before the guests arrived.

The first show in the Cabaret Room was scheduled to start at 8:30 p.m. Patrons who would eat before the show arrived at about 7:00 p.m. to 7:30 p.m. A waitress in the Cafe dining room stated that they had been told to be at work by 5:00 p.m. because people were aware that the place was going to be quite full, and customers would be trying to be seated as early as 5:30 p.m. to 5:45 p.m. She reported that patrons started coming in at 5:35 p.m., and that the room was full by 6:30 p.m. She estimated later that over 200 people had been in that room. She further related:

Waitress: *. . . . But then as showtime progressed, these people that are coming to see a star attraction, they get nervous and they want to leave — they want their dinner now, they want to get up, they want to go. By a quarter after 8, the dining room started emptying out. We left, because the show was not going to start for a while, but these people are so anxious to get a good seat, that they all have to go.*

Questioner: *So by 8:15 then, the dining room was pretty well empty.*

Waitress: *Yes sir.*

Questioner: *Now what would be your routine from there?*

Waitress: *We start pitching in and helping the busboys because we know it's a heavy load, we start reseating our stations, getting ready for more customers. And that's what we were doing and they started seating more customers, and there was a party of twenty that was just being seated.*

Customers were continuing to arrive at the Club throughout the evening, as some were planning to see the show without having dinner. At about 8:30 p.m., 8:40 p.m., 8:45 p.m., and even at 8:55 p.m., customers were arriving to eat before attending the second show.

By show time, most of the dining rooms had emptied out, customers had been directed to the Cabaret

RECONSTRUCTION OF A TRAGEDY

Room, and they had been seated or were waiting in line outside the Cabaret Room to be seated. There was also a line of customers waiting to be seated in the Garden Rooms. A Garden Rooms hostess stated that, "All the people for the second seating were just beginning to come in so I really hadn't started seating anybody yet but I still had a line of maybe forty feet of people. . . ."

A wedding party that had been in the Zebra Room had left the Club at about 8:00 p.m., or a few minutes thereafter. A cleaning woman opened the doors to the Zebra Room and checked the room. The time is not documented, but she reported that the show had just started. She stated:

> • I went in (to the Zebra Room) and I turned up the main big light. See we have two big lights to turn up to see, but these little bitty ones was all around the side. So I went over and turned up the big ones, to see how dirty the floor was. So I said, 'I'll just bring my sweeper being as they left and gone to the show, and I'll just put my sweeper in here and nobody will bother it.'

Questioner: *You turned the lights up with the dimmer switch?*

Cleaning Woman: *No. The lights I turned on were turned off, and I turned them all the way on with a switch. They have those roll-on switches. I rolled it all the way up.*

Questioner: *Then you backed out of the Zebra Room and closed the doors?*

Cleaning Woman: *Right.*

Questioner: *At that time you did not smell or see any smoke whatsoever.*

Cleaning Woman: *No sir.*

> • ... So I went around to get the sweeper and I thought, 'Oh, boy, there ain't nobody out here, I can go in and check the men's and ladies' restroom.' The ladies' restroom ain't bad, but the men's, you know. So I went in and there wasn't nobody in there at all. So I picked up a couple pieces of paper and came back out and went into the ladies'. And the bar was still lit and people was still at the bar.

The models in the dressing rooms above the Zebra Room were waiting for the other guests to finish eating to begin the fashion show. One of the models stated that there was a separate air conditioning unit in the room, and commented that the area above the Zebra Room was unusually warm . . .

Questioner: *. . . . And so you were directly over the Zebra Room then or almost directly over the Zebra Room. Did you notice any change in the temperature of the room while you were there?*

Model: *I didn't because well because they turned up the air conditioning because they said it was hot in there and well at first I thought it was hot because we were rushing around so they turned the air conditioning up and it cooled off and then (another model) she was saying, 'Boy it sure is hot in here. . . .' The air conditioning was up very high because like when you had gone outside of the door you know it seemed like it was twice as hot, right outside the door, but I think due to the air conditioning being on and we were then like I said half-dressed anyway so it was cool to me, but it was after they had turned the air conditioning up.*

The crowded conditions in the Cabaret Room have been verified by numerous patron and employee statements. Tables were situated close together, aisles between tables were narrow, and chairs were located in aisles in some areas and on the ramps. A waitress in the Cabaret Room stated:

> • . . . . and here I come into the room and I had two trays and I had a busboy behind me carrying a third tray. Well, I couldn't get through on the second level because sometimes, they're seated six chairs up there at those tables, there were eight chairs at those tables that night, and you couldn't get through. So we had to walk across the third level to go down on the steps on the second level to go on down to the first level in order for me to serve my drinks. Well also on the second level there were tables, not tables, there was just chairs there with people in them that was obstructing the way to get through but you just had to walk through them. . . .
>
> The ramp leading from station eight, which in the Pit that night, there were eight stations. Four on one side and four on the other. On my side station eight there was a

> ramp leading up from station eight from the stage up to the restroom area and it was just jammed full of chairs. You couldn't move through there.

Close to 9:00 p.m., customers were still arriving, and lines of people were in the front foyer at the reservations desk waiting to be seated. The total number of occupants in the Club is estimated to have been between 2,400 and 2,800. The total number of ocupants in the Cabaret Room is estimated to have been between 1,200 and 1,300. The estimated number of occupants in each area of the Club at the time of the fire is listed in Table 2.1. (See also Figure 8.)

Table 2.1 Estimated Number of Occupants* In Each Area of the Club at the Time of the Fire**

Cabaret Room	1,200 to 1,300
Garden Rooms	200 to 300
Empire Room	375 to 425
Cafe dining room	100 to 125
Main bar and foyer	100 to 125
Zebra Room	— to —
Viennese Rooms	100 to 125
Main north-south corridor	75 to 100
Crystal Rooms	210 to 250
Kitchen	40 to 50
Total	2,400 to 2,800

*Estimated number of occupants is less than has been previously reported, based on information in employee transcripts that many patrons had left for the 8:30 p.m. Cabaret Room show, and dining room patrons who would attend the second show were just starting to arrive. Numbers are based on the reported numbers of people in each room, adjusted to reflect the total number of transcripts and responses to questionnaires received by the Commonwealth of Kentucky.

**These figures are not intended to reflect how many people were allowed in a room or how many may have been put in the area in the past; they reflect how many were there at the time of the fire.

DISCOVERY, ALARM, EVACUATION

Between approximately 8:45 p.m. and 8:50 p.m., Beverly Hills Supper Club employees discovered a fire in the Zebra Room. Some employees alerted the Club hostess to the fire, and other employees raced to the kitchen to notify the management. Two of the managers, in turn, ran to the Zebra Room and attempted to fight the fire with the Club's fire extinguishers. Busboys and waiters assisted in the attempt to fight the fire, and ran to the kitchen for more extinguishers. Patrons in the main bar became aware of the fire and began to exit out of the Club's front doors.

Following this activity, one of the managers ordered the Club's hostess to evacuate the patrons. Various rooms were notified to leave the building at about 9:00 p.m. or a few minutes thereafter. The fire department was notified at 9:01 p.m.

Patrons in the Crystal Rooms on the second floor did not become aware of the fire until they saw smoke coming up the main, curved stairway. Once the main, curved stairway had filled with smoke, the occupants of the Crystal Rooms had only a narrow service stairway to the kitchen for their escape; two occupants on the second floor of the Club had no alternate means of exit, and were trapped or overcome in the dressing rooms and perished.

The Cafe dining room occupants saw the smoke and exited. The Viennese Rooms, Empire Room, and Garden Rooms occupants were notified almost simultaneously by Club employees, and they exited by various means.

The Cabaret Room occupants were not notified to exit until the majority of the other occupants had left the building. Their notification came at approximately 9:06 p.m., when a busboy went up on the room's stage and pointed out exit locations and the necessity to leave the building. Soon after this announcement, thick black smoke and flames traveled rapidly down the main north-south corridor and filled the Cabaret Room and part of the Garden Rooms. Most of the Cabaret Room occupants who had not proceeded through an exit by that time were overcome by the smoke and toxic gases, and died.

The sequence of events during the fire, and the action taken by patrons and employees, were related in detail in the hundreds of interview transcripts that were compiled by the Kentucky State Police. The following is a nearly sequential account of events during the Beverly Hills Supper Club fire, as described by patrons and employees who were in the Club at the time of the fire and who survived the holocaust. Most of the following statements refer to specific rooms, and direction of travel is referenced by room name. (See Figure 2.)

A female reservationist sat in the "cubbyhole" adjacent to the main bar. The small area was just outside the side doors (west) from the Zebra Room, and was separated from the main bar by curtains.

The reservationist smelled smoke and investigated. She opened the doors to the Zebra Room and saw that the room was filled with smoke, which made her eyes tear. She closed the doors immediately and notified a bartender of the fire. She stated: "And I ran out to the desk and I said, '(Ken), my God, there's a fire.' " The Club hostess was there, and the reservationist told her that there was a fire. The reservationist further related:

> (Ken) ran in and saw what I saw. He quickly closed the door because it

> was so devastating. . . . the next thing I saw was (Sammy) with a fire extinguisher. He was one of the bartenders. He had a fire extinguisher. I went back in the cubbyhole. My first thought was to pick up the book (reservations book).

Questioner: *Did you actually see any fire or flame in that room?*

Reservationist: *No. All I saw was smoke.*

Questioner: *Was the smoke filling the room?*

Reservationist: *All I know is when I saw that grey billowing and it got in your eyes, I closed the door. . . .*

Questioner: *Could you feel any heat when you opened that door?*

Reservationist: *Yes. Hot, hot, hot.*

Questioner: *Did it burn your face?*

Reservationist: *Yeah. It singed my hair a little bit.*

Questioner: *Did you get any burns on your hands? Or anywhere?*

Reservationist: *No.*

At approximately the same time that the reservationist discovered the fire, two waitresses, who were sisters, were serving a party in the Viennese Rooms. There were not enough tray stands available, so they went to the Zebra Room to get more tray stands. One of the waitresses said:

> I saw some smoke in the front bar, and thought it was peculiar, but I went on to the Zebra Room anyway, when I opened the doors the smoke just roared out at me, so my sister . . . held the doors shut while, I went after (two of the managers). I couldn't find them so I went running to the kitchen and told (another employee), (one of the managers) must have heard me, so him and one of the busboys . . . grabbed the fire extinguisher and asked me where so I told him the Zebra Room, then I went to look (for?) my sister and get out.

Another of the four bartenders working the front bar stated:

> We just got word that the show was about to start which was something on to a quarter to nine or so, and then I heard this gal, waitress came and said, 'Call the fire department.' Smoke was coming out of this hallway area, by the Zebra Room. We called the fire department. (Sammy), the bartender, he went down the hallway with the fire extinguisher, got the fire extinguisher went down the hallway, then came back and the waitresses were coming out of the room again hollering, 'Call the fire department,' which was the second time they called it. And the smoke started coming out which was hanging over the ceiling of the hallway and the bar which was sort of grey at first. We were getting the people out and then all of a sudden it just people just starting (sic) coming up to the front lobby and we got them out the front door.

(Sammy) ran to get a fire extinguisher. By the time he got back, he stated that he couldn't get within 20 feet. He yelled to the other bartender: "Let's get the people out of here."

A customer who was in the front bar with a party of five remarked:

> . . . . Then we heard two maitre d's in the dining room, which was right behind where I was sitting, 'How do we get these people out.' One said, 'Take as many out through the main entrance as we can get take the rest through the kitchen.' I said, 'Let's get out of here.' That was my exact words but they were a little harsher. When we looked back up toward the reservation girl it was getting smoky.

A waitress was obtaining drinks at the service bar when she saw the two waitresses open the doors to the Zebra Room and the smoke start pouring from the room. She stated:

> They told me to get the people out of the Empire room, so I was the one that went up to the speaker; they were in the middle of a meeting, and they were sitting there telling me to go away. I was trying to explain to them not to panic or anything, but we didn't know whether we was gonna have to evacuate yet. But to be ready; when somebody tells you to get out, to get out. Like two seconds later there was me and the other waitress that

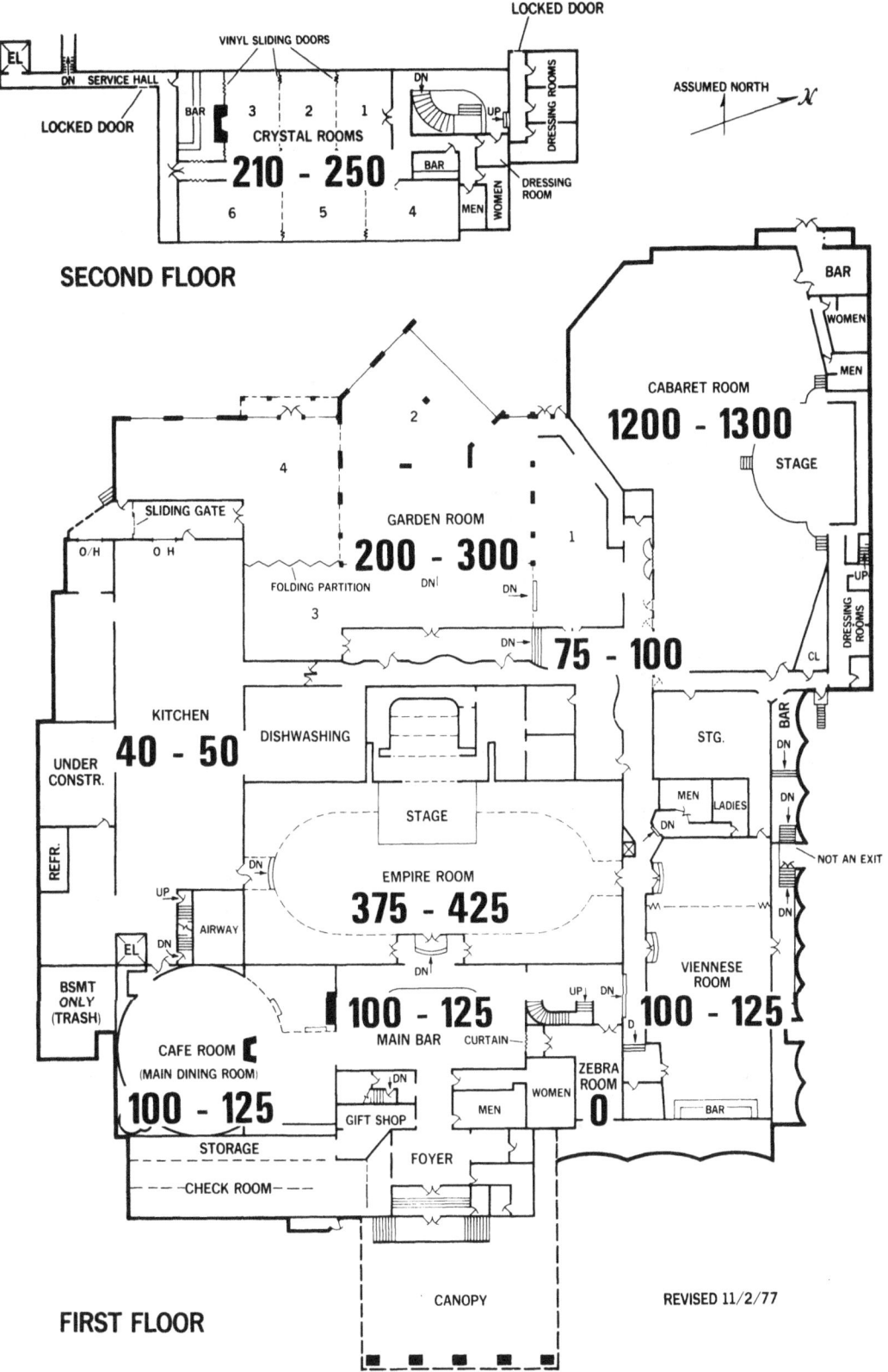

ESTIMATED ACTUAL OCCUPANCY AT TIME OF THE FIRE

Figure 8.

RECONSTRUCTION OF A TRAGEDY

> runs the front bar . . . and a bartender took them out. . . .

A cocktail waitress working at the main bar was waiting on people at her station when she saw smoke coming from the Zebra Room. She remarked:

- Well, I saw the smoke in the reflection of the mirror, but then I saw the smoke, too. It was sort of double, because of the mirror hallway and you know that type thing. I just turned around. I was walking and I turned around again. I saw (Robbie) coming out and saying there was a fire. 'Get everybody out.' So then at that point people were getting off the bar. They were sitting at the bar stools, and they were getting up and going out. I was standing right here by the Empire Room door and they were open. People were already coming out, because I think (two other waitresses) had gone back there, too, to tell them to get out.

A club hostess (Susan) told another hostess to run and tell one of the managers (Stevie) about the fire. She ". . . ran through the dining room and (Stevie) was at the other end of the kitchen, I said, 'There is a fire in the Zebra Room,' and boy he ran, you know."

Another Club hostess (Nancy) was waiting for the dining room to be reset for the 9:00 p.m. reservations when someone came up to the bar and said, "Call the fire department, we have a fire." The hostess stated:

- I immediately picked up the phone and called and reported the fire. There were people at the bar and I turned to them and told them to please leave the building that we had a fire. I then went directly into the Cafe (dining room) and started telling people to leave. Before I went to the dining room, seconds after I called the department I saw my husband (Stevie) and he shouted 'Get these people out of here, we have a fire.' When I reached the dining room I started telling people to leave. The waitresses and other hostesses were doing the same. Some people started moving and others just sat. I repeated several times that they should leave, we had a fire. I then went through the kitchen and started telling people in there. They seemed as though they already knew.

A waiter in the Cafe dining room was going back, getting silverware to reset the tables, when an employee told him there was a fire.

Questioner: *Was it an employee that told you?*

Waiter: *Right.*

Questioner: *What did you do then?*

Waiter: *I just went about doing my work. We'd had fires there before and we didn't really think much about it. Cause we'd always got them out.*

A waitress in the Cafe dining room was taking a drink order. She stated:

- I had turned around to walk away from the table, and I looked up front, which after you go to a certain point in the dining room, you could see straight up to the bar, and the hostesses stand, and the busboy started by and I said to him, 'Look at all that smoke. The exhaust fans must have gone off.' I thought this must be what had happened. And I thought, 'Well a trash can has probably caught on fire' . . . and he looked up and said, 'Yeah.'

  . . . So I started up front to see if there was a garbage (can) on fire, so maybe I could grab a pitcher of water and throw on it. And as I started up front, I noticed the smoke was a little bit thicker, so I thought, 'Boy, they've really got a garbage can going up there.' And about that time, there were customers seated in the front part of that room. See the dining room is like this. In the very middle there is a big fireplace. On this side of the fireplace, there is a service stand where you get your silverware, cups and saucers and water. You can't see all of these people seated there if you're in behind, so as I started around, people jumped up and started running. I thought, 'Gee, that's kind of dumb.' So I turned back around because a woman screamed and she jumped up and I said, 'Everybody be seated. There's nothing to worry about. Just sit down,' because I'm standing in the middle of the dining room. So everybody sat down. And a busboy . . . ran around the corner of the fireplace and said to me, 'It's not all right. The place is on fire.' I said, 'No, it's not, everybody be seated.'

> He said, 'No, . . . said the place is on fire — get everybody out.' And I still thought he didn't know what he was talking about because I've worked there too long. . . .
>
> So people jumped up again and said, 'The place is on fire.' So I said, 'Okay then, walk out, don't run.'
>
> . . . . They started toward the back. They said, 'There's an exit.' I said, 'No, you can't go that way because it's a kitchen and it's dangerous to go through the kitchen because of the floor . . . because the floor is slippery, if you're not careful, you're gonna fall, it's gonna be our fault.' So when they said, 'We can't go through the front,' I said, 'Okay, everybody go through that door, follow that door, go straight on through, back through the kitchen, there's an exit at the end of the kitchen where you can get out. Don't panic, just walk.' Because I still thought it was just smoke. So I started through and all the customers were in front of me. . . .

A patron in the Cafe dining room was with a party of twenty-two people. The party had been called from the bar and had just been seated in the rear of the room. The patron stated:

> . . . . We had just sat down. This was approximately 8:45. We had just sat down and the waitress had come around and asked us if we wanted another before-dinner drink. The people were ordering their drinks, and the waitress had left to go get our drinks, and I would imagine in a matter of minutes, we hadn't even gotten seated properly where we were gonna sit, and a young fellow came in and said, 'Ladies and gentlemen would you please leave the building, we have a slight fire.' We all proceeded to get up. I was sitting at the end of the table closest to the lounge. We got up and a waitress . . . said, 'No, it's not that much, please sit down.' So we all went and sat back down again. In a matter of minutes later again, the same young fellow came back and said, 'No, you're going to have to leave. We're going to have to evacuate the building.' So I grabbed my wife by the hand and we proceeded to leave through the lounge area, the way we came in, to go through the main entrance. We went through the dining room and got to the lounge area, and the smoke was so intense my wife started coughing and saying, 'I can't go any further.' Well, that was the only way that I knew out. I had been to Beverly Hills several times, and I said, 'We got to go this way.' So we went through the smoke up to where the lady stands and checks you in for your reservations, and we couldn't go no further cause there was too many people. They were just crowding out that door. My wife and I couldn't take the smoke so we turned around, and my party was following me, and I said, 'We can't get out this way, just turn around and go back.' So we went back in the main dining room.
>
> . . . . The main dining room had no smoke at all, maybe a mist, but no heavy stuff.
>
> . . . . one of the head girls . . . was standing in the back saying, 'Come on, go out this way.' There was an exit through the kitchen. So by that time, my whole party had gone and my wife and I were the last ones. In fact, before I went out the door, I said to (the hostess), 'Come on, get the hell out of here.' She said, 'No, I am not leaving until I make sure everybody is out of here.' I said, '. . . everybody is out of here, we're the last ones.' She says, 'No, there might be some more people coming through here.'

Meanwhile, at the other end of the Beverly Hills Supper Club (the north end, farthest from the main bar and front entrance), another employee was working in the middle Garden Room — Garden Room 2 — and was standing in the outside hall waiting for customers for the second show. He stated that (Robbie) one of the managers . . .

> . . . was in the hall with us, and two waitresses came up and notified him that there was a fire, and his eyes got real big and he started running. . . .
>
> He said, 'Where' . . . and they said, 'The Zebra room,' so he ran like hell through the back hall.

Questioner: *Now did you follow him?*

Employee: *Yes that's right.*

RECONSTRUCTION OF A TRAGEDY

Questioner: *Now then what happened?*

Employee: *And he got to the Zebra Room and there was some smoke coming out of the cracks of the doors but the doors weren't open and I don't know if he grabbed a fire extinguisher on the way or not.*

Questioner: *And what did you do, did you stay there?*

Employee: *When I saw that it was actually a fire I just stood a few seconds then I figured that we had (to?) start trying to get people out.*

Questioner: *Then where did you go?*

Employee: *I went back to the Garden Rooms stopping at the door of the Cabaret Room on the way to notify the hostesses of the Cabaret Room that there really was a fire and then they ask me how bad and I said that I didn't know that it looked like a small fire to me they ask me if I would find out.*

Questioner: *On this notification do you remember who you told that or who was you talking to?*

Employee: *It would have been (Cathy).*

Questioner: *(Cathy), would you know her last name?*

Employee: *No, I don't she was a hostess, she wasn't really a Cabaret room she was the one that set people in the Cabaret room.*

Questioner: *She was a hostess.*

Employee: *She was a hostess for the Garden Room, they stood there at that point.*

Questioner: *After you notified (Cathy) then where did you go?*

Employee: *Back to the Garden Room to get the diners in there.*

Another waiter, who was working in the Garden Rooms, was standing in the back hall. He stated:

- It's a little hall outside the Garden Room, you know. A service hall in the back of the kitchen. It leads you to the kitchen, it leads you to the Garden or it leads you over on the side where the fire started. I was standing in the hall and I saw this waitress come running down the hall. She was running and I asked her what was wrong and she told me it was a fire. And then I went down to the hall and looked down the hall and you could see the smoke was coming down the hall so I just went right on out through the Garden with the rest of the help and the rest of the people.

In the Empire Room, the Greater Cincinnati Savings and Loan League Convention was holding a banquet dinner. The group had finished dinner, and individuals at the head table were announcing awards. One of the group stated:

- A waitress came in the room, two waitresses, and one walked up to the gentleman handing out the awards and said something to him. He, in turn, turned to the guy up on the podium talking and I guess told him the same thing. He announced there was a small fire in the building and that we would please exit out the front. At that point, we all got up calmly. I didn't notice anybody running or jumping or anything. We went toward the front door of the Empire Room (south, toward the front exit). At this point, they opened those doors and we couldn't even see the bar because of the smoke. (Another couple) were in front of us, and they had gone out that door, at this point, they said you couldn't see nothing out in the barroom. The bar is only about ten feet from that door. They were the last two out those doors. They shut the doors. He said they locked them, I don't know. He said he tried to get back in that way because he couldn't see. He said they shut them and he couldn't get back in. I don't know if he could or couldn't. They exited us out toward the kitchen, the exit on the other side (west side) of the room. That would be the farthest from where I was. To the front door and then to the side door and out the kitchen.

Another patron in the Empire Room related the following events that occurred after the announcement was made to leave the room.

Patron: *As we were going, they had started us out these doors and closed the doors, and there was still a lot of people . . .*

Questioner: *You pointed to the doors entrance to the bar?*

Patron: *To the bar right. Then we started out the doorway going into the kitchen and as we*

(Continued on page 27)

THE BEVERLY HILLS SUPPER CLUB FIRE

The following photographs were taken by Joseph LaLonde, a patron who was in the Cabaret Room prior to the Beverly Hills Supper Club fire. Upon notification of the fire, Mr. LaLonde and his party left the Club. He then documented the progress of the fire from the southeast corner of the Club. The following selection of Mr. LaLonde's color photographs has been chosen to show the evacuation of the Club and the progress of the fire at significant intervals.

The first photograph taken after Mr. LaLonde exited from the Club. Shown is the southeast exit from the Cabaret Room, referred to as Exit B. People in the photograph are believed to be still exiting from the Cabaret Room. The estimated time for this photo is between 9:05 p.m. and 9:10 p.m.

RECONSTRUCTION OF A TRAGEDY

This photograph shows the canopy and front entrance to the Club. Note that fire fighters are on the scene. The illumination seen in the picture is from the lighting outside the Club; fire is not visible. The estimated time of this photograph is 9:15 p.m.

This view of the southeast exit from the Cabaret Room — Exit B — was taken at approximately 9:20 p.m. It is assumed that persons who exited from the Cabaret Room under their own power are out of the Club at this time. People seen in the photograph around the exit are believed to be attempting to rescue victims from the fire.

This is a view from the southeast corner of the Club. Note that the canopy is visible. Smoke is emitting through the top of the false front, or facade, through an area between the original outside wall of the Club and the facade. The recessed area to the lower right of the photograph, where some people are standing, is not an exit. Estimated time for the photograph is 9:30 p.m.

THE BEVERLY HILLS SUPPER CLUB FIRE

This photograph, taken at approximately 9:35 p.m., is an interesting contrast with the earlier view of the front entrance to the Club. The change in smoke conditions is believed to be due to the fire having self-ventilated through the roof.

Another view of Exit B at the southeast corner of the Cabaret Room, taken at approximately 10:00 p.m. This is the first photograph that shows a slight glow above the roof, indicating that the fire had burned through the roof. Note the smoke seeping from the roof line along the east wall of the Cabaret Room, seen in center right.

This view is from the driveway to the Club, taken at approximately 10:05 p.m. This photograph clearly shows the fire ventilating through the roof.

A view of the Club from the highway, taken at approximately 10:20 p.m. Note that the fire has spread through major portions of the building. About an hour after this picture was taken, there appeared to be a danger of building collapse, and all fire fighting and rescue personnel were ordered out of the building.

the group I was with, we were about the last to leave the room, as we were going through this door into the kitchen they opened the door over on the side of the room where we were sitting and there were people standing out there it looked like they were waiting to direct them through our room. There was a lot of smoke in that hallway.

Questioner: *A lot of smoke coming in the door to the east the east door of the Empire Room?*

Patron: *Right.*

Questioner: *That's where you first saw smoke?*

Patron: *Right.*

Questioner: *How did you go out then?*

Patron: *They started us through the kitchen and some people they directed straight through the kitchen and the rest of us they turned down this long hallway going into the Garden Room. We went into the Garden Room down a stair or two then out the door, like on the right hand side, and out into the garden. By the time we got to this door it was filled with smoke.*

A bartender in the Empire Room was requested to get two bottles of champagne. He left the Empire Room prior to the announcement of the fire, and related the following:

- ....*so I just went right through the doors and into the hallway there (presumably, the main north-south corridor) and a waitress came running and said, 'Don't let anyone go up that way.' So, I stopped all the people from going that way then I ran out that way to see what was going on and I seen one of the waitresses standing there and she opened up the doors, she was standing in front of the doors of the Zebra Room, she opened up the door and black smoke came rolling out and she shut the door and then (Robbie) was running up the hallway as I was running back down. My first instinct was to go back to the Empire Room. So, that's where I went. As soon as I went into the room there was sort of a disturbance, you know, I guess, just the atmosphere of it all, and some of the people started standing up. One of the bartenders I was working with. . . . He started out through the front entrance that goes out into the front bar. People naturally started following him*

The Empire Room as seen on the night of the fire. The Greater Cincinnati Savings and Loan League Convention banquet dinner is in progress. George Mayhew, a professional photographer who took this photo, also took photos from outside the Club after he had exited from the building.

> because that's where they came in at. He opened up the double doors, the smoke had already been into the front bar and they'd started coming in that way. Some people still tried to go through that way. So, I'd made it over to the side of the kitchen by then and I just yelled for the people to follow me and so they did. I took them out through the kitchen. I had to move trays and dinner warmers and stuff like that to make more room 'cause there was people coming down the wooden steps from upstairs over that end. So, there was a lot of people going through the kitchen.

On the other side of the Zebra Room, at the southeast corner of the building, a busboy was starting to serve people in the Viennese Rooms. He said:

- > (Another busboy)... walked up the hall and told me there was a fire in the Zebra. So I took my tray of fruit cups and sat them down on a gold chair and I told everybody in Viennese 1 and 2 to evacuate....
  >
  > I said, 'There's a fire. There's a fire in the Zebra Room. Would you please evacuate,' and I moved them out as quickly as I could.
  >
  > .... And they went out that first door, the one nearest the Zebra. And they went out the front. And they all got out safely.

Questioner: *They went by the Zebra Room out by the front bar, out the front door?*

Busboy: *Right.*

Questioner: *And so the fire in the Zebra Room had not accelerated or had built to the point where it had blocked that exit?*

Busboy: *Right.*

A patron in one of the Viennese Rooms was attending a private bar mitzvah party. He stated:

- > .... There was an open bar and there was a small orchestra playing dance music. We danced and we had a drink or two for the next approximately forty-five or fifty minutes, waiting for dinner to be brought in. I noticed about 8:50 the appetizer is being brought in on trays ready to be placed on the dinner tables but, it was never done because a moment or two after the first trays of appetizers were brought into the room a busboy or least an employee, in a white jacket, appeared in the doorway of one of the doorways of the Viennese Room and I happened to be standing and talking with somebody not far from this doorway and this employee said in a very calm and collected way that there was a fire and that we should evacuate immediately or words to that effect. Those weren't his exact words. We immediately moved to the doorway and into the hallway outside of the Viennese Room. I should add that before we were advised that there was a fire we had no knowledge that there was, we had smelled no smoke and seen no smoke and when we did get out of the doorway and into the hallway we immediately encountered the smoke which got thicker as we got toward the bar and toward the main exit. As we went into the hall and proceeded toward the bar and toward the main exit we noticed that there was thick smoke coming out of a room near the Viennese Room which I think may have been the Zebra Room but I am not sure. And I think I even saw some flames in there. But I am not sure. It was kind of very exciting panicking type of situation and you can't recall every fact that you might have seen at the time. But it seemed like an awful long way to the exit and all kinds of people were converging out in that hallway from all over, pushing and some women starting to scream and the smoke as I said was kind of thick at that early stage. But I remember distinctly choking and my eyes burning and so we did make it to the main exit and we did get out....

A patron in another of the Viennese Rooms was attending a party that included doctors and their wives. He did not hear the busboy's announcement to leave the room, but his wife told him to get up because there was some kind of alarm and everyone was leaving the room. He explained:

- > .... we came out of the entrance to the Viennese Room which we entered through and tried to turn left because that was the only exit we knew of (to?) the front but as soon as we turned left we saw smoke

> in that direction so we had no option but to turn right at the moment we came out we did not have anyone to direct us to go from the Empire Room or to the right but the previous doctors and their wives were directed by one personnel as I understood later, as I, evidently that personnel must have left by the time we got there we turned right and went past the Cabaret Room and so (saw?) all the people easily seated and no kind of movement we saw at that time, in fact, we stopped for a second or two to see on the stage we saw two people standing and announcing and it may be part of the show I couldn't tell. . . .

The man and his wife were then apparently directed to leave the line they were in and to exit through the Garden Rooms to the outside.

At about the same time that the previously mentioned rooms on the first floor were being evacuated, employees and patrons on the second floor became aware of the fire. A model in the second floor Crystal Rooms was in one of the dressing rooms and was warned by another girl, who pushed the door open and yelled:

- > . . . . get out get out just grab your purse and get out well half of us were undressed and so we just grabbed something and started going towards the door. But after the door was opened there was so much smoke you could hardly see then and so the only (way) I knew to leave was the way I came in which was the Spiral Staircase and out the front door so I started towards the stairs and you just had to kind of feel your way along because the smoke had gotten really heavy and I started down the stairs and then one of the other girls said to the other girl . . . she yelled, 'I can't see, I can't breathe,' so I grabbed a hold of her around the waist. . . .

Well when I was coming out I really couldn't tell who was where you really couldn't see but after she yelled I looked around and she reached for me and kind of grabbed me on the shoulder and then I just grabbed her on the waist and I couldn't even tell you who was next to us. So we started down the stairs and I had my hand on the rail to feel my way down and then I kept looking toward the floor and still holding onto her and got near the bottom of the stairs because my ankle kind of buckeled you know, knowing that I was near the bottom because you know, you just could not see that well. By that time there was such a crowd everybody was like shoulder to shoulder, so you just moved with the crowd and we went out and around the bar and then when we got to the front, near the front door and then that is when the smoke really got to me and we kind of rushed our way through to the side a little bit because we were a little bit smaller than a lot of the people, so we just slid on through, and I snatched her and we kind of went up on the other hill right across from it.

A waitress on the second floor reported that they had served one party in the Crystal Rooms and had cleared the room out. She related the following information:

- > . . . . Then I was taking food in to the second party when we started smelling smoke. I really didn't get too upset at first because things like that happen down there, fires here and there, bathrooms on fire and stuff, but I went back through the hallway and I noticed that it was coming in pretty good so I started running in the bathrooms and dressing rooms up there looking around to see if I could see where it started. When I come back in the hallway, our captain . . . came running down through the hall and asked me if I could see where it was coming from. I said, 'No, I couldn't find it.' By that time there were people in the hallway I think from both parties and they started wanting to know what was going on. We was trying to tell them to keep calm until we could find out. Somebody had come and told us that the room underneath of us was on fire and I didn't get too upset still because it's the smallest room in the whole place. . . .
>
> . . . . We were trying to tell the people to keep calm, that it was a fire downstairs. Before we knew it, I mean it just come up so fast it was just like a tornado. Kind of like a gust of wind. Smoke just started pouring in from everywhere and it happened so fast we just didn't have time to think. I mean in a matter in just seconds the whole upstairs was covered and we were all gagging and choking, and we were trying to show them how to get back through the

hallway into the little room that we stay in back there that goes down to the kitchen. I think people were really starting to panic because everything commenced so fast. I had grabbed one of the napkins that we use to cover my face up, and our captain was telling everybody to try to cover their face. I mean they were really getting sick quite fast, and we went back into the cubbyhole and we kept calling out . . . one of the waitresses I work with, kept calling out into the room, 'Is everybody out, is everybody out?' She was trying to make sure everybody was out of that room. Nobody answered her so she shut off the doors to our party room to try to keep it from coming in on us. The lights had went out two times I think I remember and had come back on. But then they had went out the third time and they stayed out. It was quite dark and people were panicking and for some reason we couldn't seem to move. I guess they were just congested in the stairway because we were just at a standstill it seemed there for a while. They were trying to bust the door down that went out on the roof and they couldn't get that down. We really thought we were going to die because we couldn't breathe and I was gasping for breath and my eyes were burning so bad I couldn't even open them. One of the waiters up there . . . he grabbed onto me and kept holding me up because I was really getting sick. Everything was so dark you really couldn't see anything that was going on. Somebody said they were trying to get down the elevator door which they couldn't have done but for some reason it took a while for them to start moving through the stairway. When they did, I couldn't hardly stand up. This boy held onto me and he got me all the way down the steps and all the way back to the kitchen and on to the hill. I stayed up on the hill for a while because I was real sick and the three of us, we didn't go back around.

The Crystal Room maitre d' was in the kitchen prior to the fire. He stated:

- From the kitchen I went upstairs once or twice and then at about 9:00 almost exactly I went upstairs again and as soon as I entered the dining room, (a) waitress told me that there was a fire in the Zebra Room. I saw a small amount of smoke at the end of the hall.

  I started for the Zebra Room which was right at the bottom of the main steps leading down from upstairs but I couldn't even get to the end of the hall before the smoke poured in on us. I yelled at the top of my lungs for everyone to go to the back of the room and out the back door. One man kept coming back to try to pick up something off the floor and I finally got him out.

  I proceeded to my other room where there had been 120 people, most of these people were out and I checked the doors. At the main entrance to this room, as I opened the doors, to look in the hall I was knocked back by the heat, I ran back to the back and into the back service hall. All of the people were backed up in this hall.

  To expedite getting out I told two men to knock a door down that led out onto a roof. They couldn't get it down, the lights went out and we could hardly breathe anymore. At this time, I got myself against a wall and worked my way to the steps. At this time everyone started moving pretty fast down the steps.

  From the time I first saw the smoke until I got down to the bottom of the steps was about three minutes. I am not sure of this time.

By this time, other employees who were in the main north-south corridor, the kitchen, or in the service halls were becoming aware of the fire. A busboy had been helping out in the Empire Room and had also been in the Cabaret Room a few times during that evening. He stated that he . . .

- . . . . went in the Garden Room and then the Viennese Room, that was ready to eat and me and another busboy . . . we was carrying a tray of fruit cups down to the Viennese Room and I seen this smoke and I seen (Robbie) bent over with a fire extinguisher, and I seen (Lester) with two of them, he had two of them and I seen a couple of dishwashers, my brother and a few other ones there and we went in the Viennese Room and (the other busboy) pulled out a chair and set

> the fruit cup in the chair and we ran back out to the Zebra Room and they was calling the fire department so we started evacuating everybody. I went into the Viennese Room, there wasn't nobody in the Zebra Room and to my knowledge. I went to the Viennese Room and me and (the other busboy), we told the people in there that they should leave in a very calmly (sic) manner so they left. . . .
>
> I ran back out and to the Zebra Room and the doors were on fire and the people coming outside, the upstairs party was running down into the fire and I was at the bottom of the steps, I was telling them to go up the steps and there was another busboy on top . . . he was pushing them down that way and then the mate (sic) Captain he was pushing them down into the kitchen and (another employee) was showing them the way out from there.

A waitress who was serving a group of customers in the Garden Rooms had just taken their drink order. She walked back to the kitchen through the employee hallway, and she saw a busboy running down the hall with a fire extinguisher. The waitress stated:

- This was about two minutes after nine I would say. Then I just walked into the kitchen. . . . So when I walked into the kitchen I heard someone say, 'There is a small fire in the Zebra Room, but there is a lot of smoke so evacuate everyone.' At this time like the bartenders and some of the cooks were starting out the rear kitchen door. That was the door I was coming. I could see like in the far end of the kitchen people, there was already a woman and a trail of people behind her starting in, customers. I had thought these were from the front dining room but later I found out these were probably the people from the second floor who had come down the back stairway. So I turned around and walked out of the kitchen back into the Garden Room, and by that time someone must have told the other employees in there also because everyone was walking around telling everyone to leave. There couldn't have been more than fifteen tables actually filled at that time because that was the slow time. All those people got up. It was like a big fire drill at first. . . . But everything was orderly and it was moving. . . . and then there was a steady stream of people because people were starting to come to the kitchen and out. Coming out through the Garden Room and we were standing in the Garden Room directing them to, there were two exits, but we were directing them to the exit closest, like by the hallway that led by the Cabaret Room because that was the most obvious exit from where we were. They were all lined up there. This went on maybe another minute or two. Then word got passed down the line to the employees, it's in the basement. At that point we started saying, 'Let's go, let's move, start moving people more rapidly.' They were starting to slow down at the exit so at that time a party waitress was standing in the hall outside the dining room door breaking them up as they came out saying you go this way, you go that way, so both exits were being used as these people kept coming. This maybe went on for three minutes. At the end of three minutes there weren't any more people coming through so I just went and the Garden Room was well cleared at that time. There was no customers left. I went out and just stood by the hallway outside the dining room door, just looked around to make sure no one was there. At that time I could see smoke down the hall, down the hallway that turned down by the Cabaret Room or the main hallway.

Customers at the first seating in Garden Room 2 had finished eating by about 8:00 p.m. A waiter in Garden Room 2 stated that he was serving two tables for the second show. After he had taken an order from one table, he entered the kitchen and he noted that:

- . . . . the kitchen wasn't very crowded at all because this was the slack period in between the two shows. I remember a waitress coming out of the main dining room saying, 'There's a fire, everybody get out.' It seemed too incredible to me to be true. I don't think anyone else, well, I'm not sure about that, but it didn't look like anyone else was running out when she said that. Then I saw a busboy run from this area of the kitchen.

  . . . . I saw a busboy running from the north end of the kitchen south to the main dining room doors with a fire extinguisher. And I saw two more waitresses coming through they were hollering they said, 'It's really bad, everybody get out, tell your parties to leave.' At that point I exited the kitchen through the hallway in between the cashier's office and the dishwashing room. Went down the hall, through the first set of double doors, across the hall, through a set of, through the opening to the Garden 2 Room. My parties had already been alerted by someone, maybe (another waitress), I don't know, but they were just getting up out of their seats. They had a look . . . I told them it was a fire, 'Don't panic, but you have to leave.' Everyone was leaving out the doors of the Garden Room.

In the corridor just outside the Cabaret Room, patrons who were standing in line were also made aware of the fire emergency. A male patron was standing in line in the main north-south corridor waiting to be seated in the Garden Rooms for dinner before the show. He suddenly realized that all the people who had been behind him weren't there anymore. He stated:

- . . . . Someone said something about a fire. We heard people say maybe it was just a joke. They asked if it was a fire drill. The next thing we knew all of these people were running down the hallway to the exit beside the Cabaret Room. We starting walking out slowly because we thought this was a fire practice. We heard a maitre d' said, 'Yes, it is a real fire get out.' Then he started telling everybody to get out. We walked past the Cabaret Room and they were all still sitting in there and the comedians were still going with their show. They hadn't even bothered to get out. We just started to go to the Garden Room and it was crowded at the door so we went through the bushes and were standing in the grassy area.

A husband and wife entered the Beverly Hills Supper Club with two friends at approximately 8:55 p.m., went to the reservation desk, and were directed to the bar to wait. They ordered drinks and soon were directed along the main north-south corridor toward the Cabaret Room. One of them stated:

- . . . . We got approximately two thirds down the hallway in a line the last four people in the line. We just got back there and the two people turned around and faced us and we started to talk at (sic) moment we heard footsteps running up behind me. There was a waitress and she had her forearm up and waving. 'Look out, look out,' she yelled and just a-chasing to us the doorway for the service entrance to come out in that hall to service those rooms. She ran halfway in the hall and we heard her yelling, 'Fire extinguishers, fire extinguishers.' At that point she also stopped them and told the busboy who was right behind her to check the other rooms.

The two couples had difficulty deciding whether to exit forward (north) or to return to the front of the building (south), in the direction they had come.

- . . . . we did turn around and go back out to the bar room and in entering the bar room the bar room was full of smoke and there was mass exits that time out of the bar room. It wasn't too bad for the first fifteen feet and then got quite heavy and I was very concerned because I knew I had to make it to the head bar before I could have a clear shot out the door. Which is what happened. We did make it there and the smoke started getting heavier and heavier and I told my wife to bend down to get lower, try to get underneath it. All the while I was looking up out of the corner of my eye and trying to keep my eye on the exit sign. That exit sign. I had to see that exit sign. Just about the time I broke to the head bar there. I did see the exit sign. The smoke was quite heavy, so heavy it was . . . turning over in big cotton balls I guess you would say. I have been having problems with breathing anyway because of the asthma all my life. The smoke was affecting me faster than most people. We did proceed and I was holding my breath a little bit from time to time kind of breathing a little bit at a time in short. We proceeded in file out. On getting out to the steps we had to separate and by the time out the steps maybe about a hundred feet down the steps and turned around I would say at that point I saw no more people we were the last of the people coming out. At that point I saw no more people coming

> out of the front entrance the rest the night. Either being carried out or walking nobody came out that. So I assumed we were the last 30 percent to come out of the people to come out of the front entrance. Look like there might have been 4 or 5 or 6 hundred people already out in the parking lot.

A hostess in one of the Garden Rooms was notified of the fire by a waiter and another hostess. The two hostesses went back to the garden doors, opened the doors, and "fixed them so they would stay open." The Garden Room hostess then went into the hallway and told the people waiting there that there was a fire and to exit out the doors. She said:

> • .... and we got everybody out of the Gardens that were eating dinner. ... And I got them all out and all those rooms were empty, and the waitresses were out and I turned around and I was just walking out the door and (Nancy) grabs me.... (Nancy was trying to find her daughter and husband.)
>
> .... She was starting to get hysterical. She was saying, 'I'm going to go back in. I've got to find (Christine and Robbie).' I told her, '(Nancy), you can't do that, the place is on fire.' And she said that she was definitely going to go. And I said, 'Well if you're gonna go, I'm gonna go with you.' And she said, 'OK.' So we ran, I don't even know the length of time, I know it couldn't have been long, but we ran down the hallway past the Cabaret, and I don't remember hearing or seeing anything in the Cabaret, but you know, I kind of ran by. I know there was absolutely no one in that hall at all. We looked into the Viennese Room and nobody was in there. We got all the way down to maybe — the doors to the Empire are on the right hand side and about halfway between there and to the Zebra Room, we got to there. And there was smoke just beginning to really come out of the room and there were several kitchen boys standing there with fire extinguishers running out of it. And they started screaming at us to get the hell out of the place. They were coming out of the Zebra, well I don't know as they were coming out, but they were around the Zebra Room, right around the doors, and smoke, really it seemed just beginning to come out. And they were starting to run away from it because the smoke was pouring out and you really couldn't see any flames or anything, the smoke was too thick, you know, blackish-gray. So (Nancy) and I kind of back-tracked a little bit and went through the Empire Room. And the Empire Room was completely empty except for one waitress that was yelling for us to get out. Then I ran to the Empire doors that lead into the Bar Room and I opened them maybe about 6 inches and I couldn't even see anything, the room was just completely black and smoke came in the door, so I closed it and grabbed (Nancy) again and ran on through the Empire Room and into the kitchen. And in the kitchen, there were a lot of people in there and nobody was really excited or anything, they were all just filing out through the kitchen doors into the Gardens. And I told (Nancy), I said, 'I'm going to wait in this line,' and I grabbed her and we ran around like where all the dishwashers are, there's another way you can get through into the garden. And so, we ran around there because nobody was standing there blocking the way and into the Gardens and out. As we were running out the door, like that time we had just run through the Empire Room and through the kitchen, as we were running out the same doors that I had gone out earlier, the smoke was already pouring out, because I walked right into it and I guess it came up to maybe about my chest. Well, it came down to about my chest. Well it came down to maybe about my chest. It was that low. It was fairly low already. And I walked into that and then I ran out the door. And I guess we weren't about 50 to 100 yards from it and it seemed like flames were already starting to come out that same door.

A busboy was walking down the hall when a waitress told him that the Zebra Room was on fire. He looked at the double doors (to the Zebra Room); although they were closed, smoke was coming through the top edge of the doors. He ran into the bar and told the bartender to leave: "... there's a fire in this room and you got to clear out." He then ran back down the hall to the Cabaret Room. He told a male employee, who was acting as a host at the head of the lines waiting to get into the Cabaret Room, to open some doors. The busboy then moved the rope divider and hostess stand from the corridor, and he told the people that were waiting in line to walk down the hall to the Garden Rooms area.

The busboy then walked into the Cabaret Room, proceeded down the middle aisle, and climbed onto the stage, where one of the performers handed him a microphone. He faced the patrons and spoke:

> • The first thing I did was I ask them to look at the exit sign turn around and look at the back and you will see a green exit sign I want you all to notice that exit sign and I want you to look at the other corner of the room and there will be another exit sign and I want you to notice that one so I want the left side of my room to go out of the exit sign behind that I am pointing to now, I want the corner of the room, I mean my right half of the room to go out of the other exit sign in the corner of the room the green exit room, I said, 'There's a fire in the small room on the other side of the building on (sic) I don't think there is any reason to panic or rush you should leave,' so I gave the microphone back to the entertainer and....

Questioner: *What did they do, what did the people do at that point?*

Busboy: *Well, I walked down the middle aisle and I saw some people sitting in their seats and they were staring at me like I was a nut and, and a lot of people were getting up and doing what I said nobody was rushing, nobody was panicking or anything like that....*

... I jumped up on a couch, and ran down a green couch and telling everyone to go out the exit there's a long, there's a long couch down here and there's an exit I was telling everyone to go out and told them to take a right I told them not to go to the front of the building on the stage to....

Questioner: *Were you, did panic set in at some point?*

Busboy: *Ah yea panic set in when I was in the hall and I told, I went back after I told the people to turn up the lights in the light room I went back down the main hall right here instead of going back up the hall toward the fire to see if it was put out you know, so we could tell them that they could go back into the Cabaret to see the show, and I saw this big cloud of smoke coming down the hall at me real fast and I saw (Lester) running out of the smoke, I was sure it was (Lester) he's a big man and I just turned around and went to this exit over here and there were just three doors and one was locked, and I tried to bang it open with my shoulder and it wouldn't come open and I tried to unlock it it's a key lock, you know.*

One of the patrons in the Cabaret Room said that her party was seated in front of the stage. She stated:

> • .... And these comedians were performing. They were just hilarious, and we were relaxed and enjoying it, when this busboy just came on the stage, it just didn't register with people. That's all I can say. I think the comedians said something to the effect, but people just weren't moving, and they said something to the effect that this was serious, that we'll come back in a few minutes and we'll continue where we left off.

Her party then got up to leave. They exited toward the chapel (Exit A).

> • .... By that time it was crowded with people. And we could definitely smell smoke by the time time (sic) we were going out of the Cabaret Room. And as we were going down this aisle, out to the chapel that led out to the exit on the outside in the back, somebody yelled, 'Get moving!' I think it was some personnel, maybe that same boy. I looked back and then I could see the smoke coming. The people started pushing and shoving.

The party eventually made it out of the Cabaret Room through Exit A.

Another patron in the Cabaret Room related that he and his wife exited through the double doors (G) at the north end of the main north-south corridor just after the busboy had announced to the Cabaret Room audience that everyone should leave the building as quickly as possible. The patron stated:

> • .... So my wife and I started moving back toward the entrance that we had come into the Cabaret from, went into the hallway, turned right and moved along that passageway until we came out into what is known as the garden area. As we

moved down the hall, when I first came into the hall from the Cabaret there didn't appear to be any panic or a large accumulation of smoke. But as I got closer to the exit that goes out into the garden, I looked back over my shoulder and there was a tremendous amount of smoke moving down the hallway toward that exit. At that point, a man said, 'Move faster, there's people back here and smoke around us, hurry up.' So then everybody started moving at a more rapid pace. I would say at that point there was panic starting in that hallway. . . .

Everybody was moving out fine until we got in the hallway and that man said, 'There's smoke around us and you people up front move it out' — I can't recall exactly what he said — but as we were going out we could hear the two comedians on the stage talking to the people through the mikes and saying, 'When the fire is out, we'll start the show right from the beginning again. It's probably nothing to it, don't worry about it.' They were trying to keep everybody calm. But then as we got into the hallway, we could hear the two comedians say, 'Don't come up here on the stage because there's no exit back here behind the stage.' By this time, I wanted to get out, you know?

Questioner: *If you will, describe the condition of the hallway when you left the Cabaret and turned right to go down the hall. Did you look back towards the front of the building?*

Patron: *Yes sir, I did. When I first came out of the Cabaret and looked to my left, which would be toward the front of the building, I didn't see, all I could see was people moving toward me. I really didn't pay attention if there was smoke around or not. I would have realized there was smoke if it had been heavy. But I moved down the hall and as we went by the garden room, which would be on our left as we went down the hall, there was a lot of smoke in the garden room and there was busboys and waiters running around like there was no set pattern what they were going to do. Everybody was just kind of moving around. I don't know if they were trying to get people out or what. Then I looked in the garden room and saw smoke and then I looked back behind me and there was smoke coming down the hall, and it was heavy, thick, black smoke rolling down the hall. . . .*

Questioner: *After you and your wife got outside the building, how long do you think it took the black smoke to reach the exits?*

Patron: *Thirty seconds, if that long. It wasn't more than 15 feet behind me when I hit the door.*

Questioner: *Then how many people had gone out before you?*

Patron: *That would be hard to say. There wasn't a whole lot of people that had come out, and they had come from other rooms, too. I was one of the first people to leave the Cabaret room out of that exit.*

Questioner: *How long before you saw the fire?*

Patron: *Less than a minute.*

Questioner: *Then you saw no more people coming out?*

Patron: *No. That's why we were so surprised that there wasn't more than 161 dead. I told her, I said, 'There's gonna be a lot of people die in this fire.' Apparently a lot of the people behind us changed directions and went back and got out another way because there was a lot of people behind us.*

Another patron in the Cabaret Room was seated with other persons in her party to the left of the stage, "kind of over in the corner. . . . we were up fairly high." She heard the busboy make the announcement to the audience. She described the following:

> . . . . He indicated that it was on the other side of the building and there was no big rush. The comedians went on joking and said, 'Folks, we'll probably be back in a few minutes, probably nothing serious.' We got up and started walking around the tiers calmly and slowly. Everyone was doing this, to my knowledge. I guess we had gotten halfway to the exit.

Questioner: *Were you attempting to exit the north exit to the chapel area?*

Patron: *Yes. I looked back and I saw people moving down below in the bottom area. Everybody seemed very slow. I looked back again after we had maybe gotten a little further than halfway, and I saw smoke coming in to the area down on the other side of the room. I said, 'Oh my gosh.' So we started walking maybe a little faster. I looked over my shoulder again and flames were pouring through that entrance where we came in. I* *couldn't believe my eyes. We kept walking and some man down below, I remember, hollered, 'Speed it up up there,' or 'Hurry up.' So we were pretty close to the exit by then, so we kept walking faster and faster. I knew there were a lot of people behind me. It seemed to me like maybe 200-300 behind me and (Clara) was getting away from me, and I was getting worried. I kind of rushed up there. I got on the top-level tier and I almost ran to catch up with her. I knew that a couple of my friends were behind me. We got through a kind of a hallway, I guess where the bar area is, and then the door going outside was single. It was fairly wide, but it was single. We got out there. I was pretty sure I was beside (Clara). After we got out, smoke started pouring out that doorway that we had just come out. I hadn't inhaled any smoke or anything, but it was pouring out right after we came out. I couldn't believe it. We weren't a minute too soon. We got out and couldn't find (Clara's) sister. We were getting so worried. We couldn't find her anywhere. She finally tumbled out later. She had been knocked out. The people after us were just falling out of the door. I mean literally falling all over the ground. It was terrible.*

A member of the band was seated on the Cabaret Room stage when the announcement was made. He stated:

- *. . . . After it was announced the comedians stayed on for a little while to sort of direct traffic. Everybody got up and started for the exits. The band members came off the risers and walked in to the back and most of us started putting away instruments as fast as we could and then we also went out the door. I think they I think that's the south door, the back-stage small fire door (Exit B). I believe it's on the south end of the club. It's on the, it faces the same direction as the main entrance or the entrance under the portico in the front. . . .*

  . . . . That's the way we made our exit. When I left it was very orderly. In fact a gentleman let myself and (another person who was backstage) go ahead because we had a lot of equipment in our hands. She had a TV set, I had my instrument. And at that time most of the musicians were out already, all the string players, John Davidson had been informed and he was out, and a few members of the band were still packing their instruments, basically I would say the ones still packing their instruments when I left, maybe only three or four more of them actually got out. The remaining five or six are the casualties. And we quickly gathered our belongings went out that door and we went down the sidewalk along the side of the Viennese Room and then we walked a few steps to our left down on the grassy hill there and turned around to see who else would come out. We weren't there very long, I would say only maybe a minute at the very most, maybe a minute or two it is hard to tell in a situation like that, to get it exactly, because of all the excitement. But I would say not more than a minute or two, probably not that long. A huge ball of flame came out the door, and then smoke just before that, black smoke that everybody talks about. And after that I would say only a few people came through that door and then there were no more people who came out under their own power.

Another patron was seated directly in line with the middle of the stage in the Cabaret Room, two tables back from the stage. He stated:

- *. . . . The boy (busboy) took the microphone and you know, like everybody said, he did a good job, he pointed out the exits first. He told everybody calmly to leave from the exits. Made mention of the fact that there was a fire later at the end of his conversation so the people wouldn't be alarmed on the front end. Then he ran off the stage, people still weren't moving quickly enough, he got on the couch that faces the stage, pointed to all the exits again, and ask everyone to please quietly but quickly start moving. And I believe he went and had the lights turned on.*

Questioner: *Did you leave as soon as he told you there was a fire, did you start to exit then?*

Patron: *We started to get and we were in the middle of the room and of course we were at a point where we didn't know where we came as far as which exit to use. We were right in the middle. So we had a choice to make, which exit we wanted.*

Questioner: *Which one did you go out facing the stage?*

Patron: *Well, eventually. What happened was, our party of 6 since we were in the middle, people started going to one exit other people went to another and we were as far from either exit no matter which one we picked being in the middle of the room. One of the people in my party said, 'Let's go on the stage and there's got to be a way backstage.' And he and I discussed for about a moment whether to do that and I said, 'No, we shouldn't because now we're just creating another avenue of confusion for a lot of people. A lot of people might start following us and I don't think we should do that.' He said, 'Yeah but there's no other way, you know, look at the people trying to get out here.' We were the closest to the stage. So he said, 'Come on let's go this way.' I said, 'OK.' So we got on the stage and (the two comedians) were still up there talking and they told us there was no way out this way and to do what the boy said, 'Don't go backstage this way.' I said, 'OK, I agree.' Turned around and started to go toward the way that we came in. . . .*

- In other words, if you're facing the stage, we went to the right, if you're facing the stage. And either going to utilize the main entrance to the room where most of the people come or the fire exit which overlooks the hillside.* When we got to that point there was an employee there that was like a traffic cop, you know, policing or channeling people away from that area. He said, 'Don't go this way.' And he pointed to the other side of the room, you know, he motioned to go to the other side of the room (Exit A) and from which later putting it all together that the smoke was more intense at the exit that he was steering people away from and that's why he was doing it. . . . what he was doing. So we started to follow his directions and go to the other side of the room. And as we walked around to the other side I mean there was a lot of people trying to get out that one door that takes you to the chapel (Exit A). We were last in line for that line since our indecision plus we were in the middle of the room anyway and we (were) exactly last, our party of 6. We started to go that way and my girlfriend and another person of the party said, 'We won't ever get out this way,

---

*Presumably, they traveled toward the south end of the Cabaret Room to use either the exit at the southwest corner of the room to the main north-south corridor, or the exit (Exit B) at the southeast corner to the outside.

look at the people trying to get out there.' We were unaware at the time about the other door going to the Garden Rooms which probably was the safest way out. I mean I never even gave that one any thought. The first thing I saw was people going towards that exit that led to the chapel. We started up that way and then realizing that if there was any fire of any magnitude we were too far in back of that line to evacuate and get out. So we traced our tracks and went back the original way we were going which was where the busboy told us not to go and we went that way and he said, 'Don't go this way it's not safe,' and I said, 'Well, it's not going to be safe the other way either,' so we disobeyed his orders or his suggestions and we started out the tiers, facing the stage to the right, and followed that exit sign (toward Exit B), you know, and we got up there, we were in the back of that line also by this time, but that line was shorter than the other line and that's the only reason we picked it. . . .

We got up to the corridor, by that (time?) there was a lot of smoke, we got in the corridor and I don't know (how?) long the corridor was when we made a left and we saw that exit sign and we made a left and the smoke was very, very, you know, it got in my throat and my lungs, and we were all coughing and it was very dark there because of the smoke and we just kept on going until finally we saw the door open, the door was open, I could see the light outside, I could see the Beverly Hills neon sign out there, and I knew we were out. In the corridor there wasn't too many people behind me because like I said most of them were going the other way. There was a few people behind me. There was very little shoving. The shoving was of a constructive shove. It was shoving to move people faster, you know, you can move faster if someone's pushing you a little bit, helping you out, there was no like destructive type of thing where you just taking people away and going in front of them or anything like that. It was orderly. I kept talking the whole time we were in the corridor telling people to stay calm, don't panic, don't anybody push or hurt anybody else. And I just kept doing that in the corridor. My girlfriend,

> she had her face in my back so that she wouldn't breathe in any fumes. I got a lot of smoke in me. How much I don't know. How much more I could have taken, I don't know. It didn't seem like we'd go too much further, you know, and we got out.

The patron related that another couple in his party had gotten out first and . . .

> . . . . when we got out there he said, 'Did you see the smoke coming out. The smoke, the fire I mean, came out with you. The flames.' I said, 'No I didn't see any flames.' My girlfriend kept commenting how hot, the intense heat, you know, on her back, which was probably the flames. He claims he saw flames shoot out the door at that point coming right behind us. In fact, he thought we were on fire. They were above our head and behind us. So apparently at that particular time there couldn't have been too many more people come out that door. That's the door facing the hillside with the steps (Exit B).

A bartender who had been in the Crystal Rooms on the second floor, and had exited to the outside, returned to one of the Cabaret Room exits. However, it is not clear from his statement whether he was referring to Exit A or Exit B. He stated:

> And that was, there was no question in my mind about how serious this thing was at that point because people were just stacked up and they were alive you know. Maybe they still are I don't know but there were maybe five or six bartenders that I worked with at one time or another and they were getting as many as they could get out of there.
>
> . . . . there was a woman . . . and she was out of this thing except there was about six people, there was enough people where we couldn't get her out at this time because they were on her legs, the back of her legs, she was clear of this thing but she had all this weight on her and we just about pulled her eyes (sic — arms?) out of their sockets and we couldn't move her. And then there was man that was (on) top, he was a heavy guy and he was reaching his arms up and so I thought he was all right and he looked like he was on top and that was the first thought, get him off top so you can do something with the bottom ones and anyway I had him wrap his arms around my neck and I pushed up against this door as hard as I could and I moved the guy about this far, about two feet and about this time he was out (of?) it, he didn't have much strength to help me and I didn't have enough strength to lift him and he just looked at me and shook his head you know, there was nothing I could do and then there was a young girl, she was (on) top and she was alive and well and everything else, she wasn't screaming or anything but she was in fine shape, and I started to walk out with her and her leg was wrapped around a table, I don't know how that table got there but there was a table leg and her leg was wrapped around it and it was just entangled in there and she couldn't pull it loose. So that's my recollection, I can't tell you the one (sic) I left there, I couldn't take any more, that's I think when I left there, it was terrible, just terrible.

A waitress in the Cabaret Room was just returning from the service bar to serve her customers:

> . . . . I must have gotten into the room just as these people had been notified that there was a fire because I didn't see (the busboy), I didn't hear him say there was a fire. The people I heard say that there was a fire was (one of the comedians onstage). He was saying, 'Ladies and gentlemen, please do not panic, there is a fire, there are exits to the right, exits to the left do not panic, we want to get you out, there is a fire.' At that point I put my trays down. It took me about ten seconds to get from the center of the stage over the first steps and (Rita) and myself were helping these old people up, we just helped a couple of old people up and we were telling them that it was a bomb scare, not to worry. Then about that time, I looked over my left shoulders, over my left shoulder, and I heard a big woosh sound. It was not really big enough to sound like a blast, but it was like some sort of big 'shor' or something. There was flame and smoke and it just rolled into the room and it was the blackest smoke I'd ever seen. The only way, if you could just take oil and just get it to roll in mid air then that was the way the smoke

was. I knew at that time, I was going to die and up until that time, everybody was orderly. There wasn't any chaos, no screaming, no panicking or anything. It was when the people saw the smoke and the fire that they became panicky and they started screaming. I knew that this was it that we were going to die. I screamed at (Rita), I said, 'My God it's for real. There really is a fire.' The people had stopped moving. It just seemed like they were kind of shuffling. I don't know if it was because of me wanting to get out so fast that made it seem that way or what. But, I knew if I didn't do something to get over those people, I wouldn't get out so I jumped up on the tables that was the only thing I could see that would be a clear path to get ahead of those people and at that time I wasn't thinking about anything but getting out of there, because the smoke was right on us. I got up to the double door, which did not lead outside, it led into another bar and I jumped down in the crowd and (Rita) jumped back into the crowd and we surged backwards and we surged forwards and when we did, I grabbed a hold (of) a man's collar. He pulled me on through and I turned around to look because the smoke and the flames were coming, the smoke was coming out of the double doors out of the Cabaret with me, right at the back of my head. There must have been flame, because my blouse was burnt. As I came out, I turned to look and the people weren't screaming any more. The smoke had covered them all up.

A view of Exit A, taken from the northeast corner of the Cabaret Room. The photo is believed to have been taken during rescue operations, and the individuals shown are assumed to be employees and other persons in the process of rescuing victims from the Cabaret Room. (Credit: Mayhew Photographers)

FIRE SERVICE AND RESCUE OPERATIONS

A Cincinnati Fire Department captain attended the Beverly Hills Supper Club on the night of the fire as a patron with his family. They arrived at the Club at 8:45 p.m., and were directed to the bar area to wait for their table. They had just obtained drinks from the bar when they were paged to be seated for dinner. They were directed through the Hallway of the Mirrors to the corridor leading to the Cabaret Garden Rooms (the main north-south corridor). The corridor was roped off into two lines; one line was for the Cabaret Room, and the other for the Garden Rooms. The captain and his party had waited in line two or three minutes when a couple of waitresses came hurriedly from the Garden Rooms area and passed by the captain, almost knocking down one member of his party. Almost immediately, the captain noticed that the waitresses were on the verge of panic, although they were trying to subdue their panic. A hostess immediately started moving the line the captain was in, and they made a left turn, a right turn, and went through the doors to the outside.

The captain asked the waitresses what was wrong, and they replied that there was a fire in one of the party rooms. The captain found a waiter and asked whether there was a standpipe in the building, but the waiter did not seem to know what the captain was asking him. The captain identified himself, and said that maybe they could put the fire out.

> So we ran back in and he showed me where it was now I don't know whether we curved back out and went through the hall that I originally came from or whether we went through a door and was cutting through the Empire Room to this room. I don't know. I know we did get beyond a doorway a second doorway other than the outside doors. It started to get dark in there and I felt heat at my head level. This is a sure indication that there is something ahead that is creating a lot of heat. Right then is when I realized that there was a fire of pretty good proportions up ahead.

At about the same time the fire fighter-patron was attempting to locate the fire,* the county dispatch center received a telephone report of the fire. The county notified the Southgate Fire Department (1300)** and the Fort Thomas Fire Department (600)** of the fire at the Beverly Hills Supper Club. One fire fighter was at the Southgate firehouse at the time the alarm came in; other fire fighters were called at home on their tone-alert radio receivers. All equipment responded.

The Southgate rescue van unit 1320 was first on the scene with Southgate Fire Chief Riesenberg, Two fire fighters, and the driver. Behind the rescue van was Engine 1301, with six fire fighters, and Engine 1302, with eight fire fighters. Ambulance 1300A also responded to the alarm, but was delayed a few minutes in waiting for additional personnel.

As the rescue van traveled south on U.S. 27 and came in view of the Beverly Hills Supper Club, the chief could see gray smoke coming out of the eaves throughout the entire length of the building, north to south. At that time, the chief radioed to Newport (900) to send their pumper as preplanned.

The Newport assistant chief had heard the initial alarm broadcast; a moment or two later, he heard an announcement for a Fort Thomas engine (604) to respond to the fire. Without waiting to be called, the assistant chief told the Newport dispatcher to hit the alarm for Engine Company 902. An engineer and two other fire fighters accompanied him, and they drove towards the Beverly Hills Supper Club. Partway there, they heard another radio dispatch for Newport to send Engine Company 901 to the fire. Engine Company 902 was already on its way, so Engine Company 901 did not respond. In total, three fire departments — Southgate, Fort Thomas, and Newport — responded on the first alarm.

As the Southgate rescue unit was proceeding up the Beverly Hills Supper Club driveway, the chief saw people coming out of the southeast exit (B) from the Cabaret Room. Upon arriving at the Club, he and either an employee or a person on the site went inside the front door just slightly. People were streaming out of the front exit and stopping immediately outside of the building, and fire fighters pushed and shoved to move people away from the front steps. The chief was able to move to the top of the steps, but could see no fire. However, he did see a tremendous amount of smoke coming out, and the smoke was starting to go low and fill the foyer. People were still pouring out from the building.

Chief Riesenberg knew that there was nothing he could do inside the building without a hose line and some help, so he returned outside. The rescue van driver and another fire fighter had also entered the front of the Club, but couldn't get very far. They exited from the building to get a hose line. When they returned to the building and entered the front door with masks on, they still could not effectively penetrate the building without a hose line. However, at that time, there didn't seem to be any more people in the front area.

At this time, either one of the managers or an employee started hollering, "People on the roof!" As some fire fighters were attempting to enter the front of the building, others put a ladder up, and four fire fighters climbed to the roof. They could not find anyone on the roof. They used an axe to open a door

---

*The official time that the county dispatch received the alarm of the Beverly Hills Supper Club fire was 9:01 p.m. According to the Southgate fire chief, the first apparatus arrived at the Beverly Hills Supper Club at 9:04 p.m. This time was estimated, as it was not logged.

**Numbers refer to fire department radio numbers, and correspond with apparatus from each department, i.e., 1301, 1302 = Southgate; 600 series = Fort Thomas.

THE BEVERLY HILLS SUPPER CLUB FIRE

The front entrance to the Club, as seen from the southeast. Fire fighting operations are in progress. (Credit: UPI)

to the second floor Crystal Rooms, but could not find anyone in those rooms as far as they could penetrate with a hose line. At about this time, Chief Riesenberg called for additional units from Wilder Fire Department (1400), and asked for Highland Heights and Cold Springs rescue squads.

Meanwhile, inside the Beverly Hills Supper Club, the Cincinnati fire captain, who was a patron at the Club, and either a waiter or a busboy had gone back into the building and moved towards the fire. The fire captain stated:

- We advanced a short distance, I'd say within about 5 seconds, I looked ahead of me and I could see about 20 or 30 feet and I could see flames and hear crackling like combustion. It suddenly the smoke just came down and it got to our level and we had to bend down and ended up in yelling. This kid started to panic, I don't know what he was saying, I grabbed him by the belt. I said let's get out. We were crawling and the heat was getting tremendous and the fire was over my head then. This is the closest that I ever came to panic. The ceiling (smoke level) at that time was I'd say about 18 to 24 inches from the floor, I must have hit this area here through a doorway or something, it was still daylight out and I could see the glass. I stood up then, the heat was tremendous, I knew I wasn't going to get off course; and we made it to these doors and we got outside. Right in here I do remember hearing people screaming, not in this area but I heard screams...

  ... I didn't know where they were coming from but I heard people. So I came out these doors and I don't know what happened to the busboy. I saw a lot of people over this way and I saw some people crawling and choking, coughing, found out later it was a stage exit or whatever. So, I didn't, I wasn't in bad shape, I wasn't coughing and stuff because I didn't have that much smoke just a little. I ran over there and the people stopped coming out, there was a lot of kitchen help over here. Black men with white pants on and tee shirts. They were putting handkerchiefs over their mouths, which is really of no protective value, and these doors were open and I believe they had panic locks on them panic bars. So the smoke was pouring out these doors approximately mid-way up from the half way point on up. I did hear screaming in there I got down in a duckwalker (squatting), I still didn't want to mess up my pants

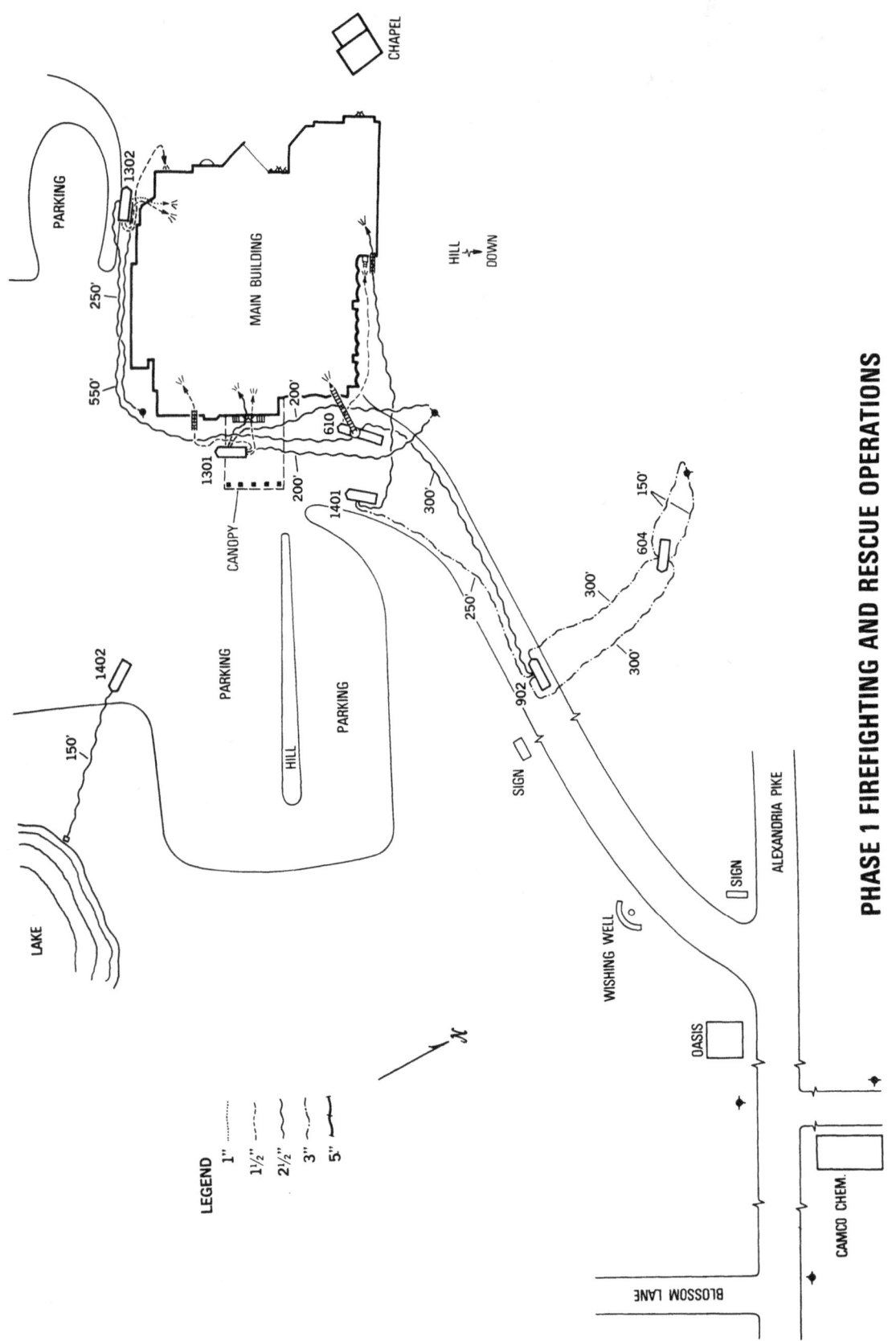

Figure 9.

which later I totally ruined, and I went in there and approximately 10 or 15 feet inside this door not straight but at an angle there was a double door but it didn't open completely, there was a partition where the two doors meet, and there I just saw a wall of heads and arms. Just people piled up right there screaming and waving their arms. I called out for a couple of those guys to give me a hand and I started pulling people just reaching heads and arms coats or anything they were piled I'd say four or five high all the way across this door. It was just a nightmare. Kept pulling them off and pulling them off finally I got to the point where I had to keep lifting up the heads of people and I was going up into the smoke and did you ever fight a fire?, it gets to you, I described this to my boy a couple of times I compared it with lifting weights you always try to get that one more, even when you can't squeeze out that one more that's when you tell your mind I'm going to do one more. I'm comparing that to this because that is what I was doing in here one more, one more. I had one woman by the arms trying to pull her out and down out of the smoke I couldn't do it I was trying to pull her horizontally, her legs must have been locked in with other people. So I stood up and reached up on her arms more and she even grabbed my arms. I tried to pull her and I just couldn't and the heat was getting intense. This is the part where I'm kind of ashamed of myself cause I had to get out. There were no firemen there yet at this time. These people, I came out coughing, and these people wanted to go in and I don't know whether they went in or not but there was quite a few people right in front of the chapel laying down coughing and everything and I went to see how they were. I heard sirens, this is what I've been saying but I don't know whether I gave artificial respiration at this time or not. . .

At the front of the Club (south side), one of the owners recognized a Southgate fire lieutenant, grabbed him, and said, "My God, we've got a situation around the side." The lieutenant led a crew of fire fighters to the east side. Other reports were received at the same time that people were trapped in the Viennese Rooms and that the fire was into the bar and off to the right. Fire fighters took 1½-inch and 2½-inch hose lines in the front door, and almost immediately a hysterical report was received from an employee in a tuxedo that people were trapped in the Cabaret Room.

The chief ordered that the lines in front be abandoned, and all available fire fighters then went around to the Cabaret Room to assist in rescue operations. The lieutenant who had taken a crew around the east side was at the chapel exit (Exit A from the northeast corner of the Cabaret Room) and was coordinating efforts to drag victims from the building. Employees had already started pulling people out before the fire fighters arrived to help.

Victims were being dragged out bodily. One fire fighter reported that he put breathing apparatus on and went in as far as he could get. However, he couldn't enter through the service doors because people were stacked in the doorway. Other victims were at the service bar, and others were lying on the floor in the hallway. Rescue operations became confused as a result of too many people getting in the way; finally the rescue was organized, with seven or eight fire fighters pulling victims to the exit door, and employees taking these victims from the exit door away from the building.

As other apparatus responded to the fire, the first unit from Fort Thomas — an engine — connected to the hydrant at the bottom of the hill. The Fort Thomas chief requested the Fort Thomas aerial as soon as he arrived on the scene.

Before other apparatus arrived, Southgate had only small lines into the kitchen area from unit 1302 that were fed from the hydrant at the southwest corner of the Club. However, this was known to have a low volume water flow.* When the Newport engine arrived, it was moved halfway up the driveway and pulled over to the driveway's side as closely as possible. Two, 3-inch hose lines were pulled from the engine down over the grassy slope, and hooked to Fort Thomas's engine (604). They had water coming from Fort Thomas, and were waiting for somebody to drop a hose line as they went up the hill in order for them to supply water.

Shortly thereafter, two pieces of apparatus came up the driveway. It is believed that the Fort Thomas aerial was first and that it dropped either a 2½- or 3-inch line. Two more engines from Wilder went up the driveway. The second engine dropped a line off; a few minutes later, a second line was connected to the Fort Thomas aerial. That second line was run to the Wilder engine, which was located just south of the Fort Thomas aerial. (See Figure 9.)

---

*Fire fighters had preplanned the Beverly Hills Supper Club just two weeks prior to the fire, and were aware that this hydrant would flow only 170 gpm at 0 psi.

The Newport assistant chief released his captain and engineer after they had water, to assist at the scene. The assistant chief was operating the engine himself, and up to that time had not become aware of the magnitude of the tragedy in the Cabaret Room. A former apparatus company representative who had been at the Beverly Hills Supper Club with his wife came down the driveway and told the assistant chief that there were people trapped in the Cabaret Room. He did not have any idea how many were trapped, but he mentioned something to the effect that it was just horrible up there.

The assistant chief asked the representative to take over the engine operation so that he could go up to the Club. Although the former manufacturer's representative had not yet located his wife, he relieved the assistant chief. The assistant chief ran into a member of the Fort Thomas Department, and the two of them took approximately 200 feet of 1½-inch hose off one of the engines. They went through the front of the building and made it inside the doorway (where the main bar is) as their line was charged. However, because all air cylinders were being used, they did not have breathing apparatus. The assistant chief stated:

- ... we went through the front of the building and we got just inside of the doorway where the main bar is and they charged our line and over here to the right which would be the Zebra Room you could just see the fire burning. Over here to the left which I assume the main dining room the big dining room over there on the left it was burning there and they you could see just a glow in the Empire Room. I mean you know it was so full of smoke that you could just see a glow in there. Now what we did was that we charged that line and we were trying to get on into the building. Now out here at the doorway I don't know where this line came from but there was an inch and half line laying on the floor out there but it only went into the building I say approximately maybe thirty or forty feet. And we hollered out to somebody to put an extension on that hose so that we could penetrate into the building further cause what we were worried about is that this thing was burning above us. We could hear it burning, evidently on the second floor up there and the parapet itself up underneath that was burning, because somebody outside with a pipe pull (pike pole) trying to pull that down and I think that they had a booster line or something out there. I am not sure I don't think that it was an inch and half hose. But we were worried about getting in here and having this thing fall down behind us and get trapped and we wanted to get somebody to put some more hose on there and get in there with us. This was not done while I was there. I was in this vicinity I would say roughly for fifteen to twenty minutes. I saw this fire over here was just getting bigger and bigger and bigger and it was burning and going toward the Cabaret.

The assistant chief then realized how serious the fire was. He also heard descriptions of people stacked two and three high in the building and hundreds of people trapped in the Cabaret Room. He decided to go to the Cabaret Room to see if he could remove any people. The assistant chief stated:

- I went to the front door and across and down the hillside to a set of steps that I found out. I had never been back in that area before. I have been in Beverly Hills for the show but I had no idea what was in the back of it as far as the exit how the stage was or anything else. When I got back there there was some bodies laying outside the building there at the bottom of the steps. Somebody had pulled them maybe 5 or 10 feet away from the steps. There were a couple firemen with masks on that was up inside the doorway. I went up to the steps* and when I went in there was a — you could make a left turn or you could make a right turn. I went in and I made a right turn and to me it seemed like it might be four or five feet then I ran into another hallway that turned to the left. I crawled down that hallway and there was a dressing room or a room. I assumed that it was a dressing room on the right side of the hall way. And I went in there and there were approximately four or five bodies laying in this room. With the help of two or three other people that was in there we pulled their bodies out, drug them down the steps laid them out on the sidewalk.

---

*The exit described was the southeast exit from the Cabaret Room, Exit B.

THE BEVERLY HILLS SUPPER CLUB FIRE

Questioner: *From the time that you entered side door and until you found those bodies. Did you come in contact with any flame.*

Asst. Chief: *Not in this rear section. I could hear flames out here. I could hear them cracking.*

Questioner: *Can you understand possibly why these people got lost. I mean why they couldn't find the door.*

Asst. Chief: *Well, there were a lot of doors back in there. Now like I said I don't know where when you went in if you took a left. I don't know where it would have taken you.*

Questioner: *Did you have a mask on.*

Asst. Chief: *No. They didn't have any more. They were all out.*

Questioner: *Yet these people — were they dead or unconscious or. . .*

Asst. Chief: *I would assume that they were dead. I don't know if they revived any of them or not. There were some doctors outside at the bottom of the steps. There were some priests out there and there were approximately 25 or 30 firemen standing out there. . . . I was crawling. I was on my belly. I crawled back this hallway and we only brought a couple of them out of there and the first time that I went in I crawled back that hallway and that is the first room that I went into and I pushed a couple cases away and I guess that there might have been as many as five more people in there. We pulled them out and other firemen drug them on out to the door.*

Questioner: *Were any of those bodies burned.*

Asst. Chief: *No. None of these people were burnt. As far as a charred burn. I mean they might have had small burns on them. As far as their clothing being burned up. No. They just looked like people that had just keeled over and maybe had had a black soot effect. You know on their face like coal dust or something.*

Questioner: *In your opinion, Chief, as a professional fire fighter was there any indication to you at that point, in that area, in the hallway or in that room, was there any indication that there had been a flash I mean other than the smoke was there.*

Asst. Chief: *I didn't see anything burnt back there. No sir. . .*

- Now that is the first room that was on the inside on the right of that hallway. Now I went back outside and got a breath of air as we were taking these bodies out. Cause it was harder than hell to breathe in there. And I was crawling on the floor. Then I went back and I went past that dressing room door and in the hallway itself there was — it looked like I was going into another room like. Straight ahead in the hallway. Is just what it seemed like to me. They were different cases, like a fellow would put a trombone in and so on and so forth and I grabbed them and shoved them back toward the room that we had just taken these bodies out of. And I crawled what looked to be like another big open area and I remember that there were closets over in the corner of this. And it just struck me funny now this would have probably have been in this area here is what I am talking about now and there were fellows in tuxedos. I can remember at least three and it struck me that they were probably members of the band. This is what I couldn't understand is why members of the band would be there when this doorway was probably 30 or 35 feet away. They surely knew how in the hell to get out of there. I found out later on that they did say that these people were members of the band. See they had their black tuxedos on and over here in the closet and what looked to me like maybe 15 to 20 people just stacked one on top of the other in this closet. Now we drug some more bodies out. We went back in and drug some more bodies out and I can recall crawling back there at least four times and just before I went back the last time. . .

The assistant chief crawled out the exit to the top of the steps. There he saw twenty to twenty-five bodies lying on the ground. He said that he "blew his lid" and screamed at a number of young fire fighters standing near the steps, "If I can get in there without a mask, you can!" He recognized a young boy that he knew who was not a fire fighter but who was there to do whatever he could, and. . .

- . . . he came into the building with me and maybe 4 or . . . of these other ones came with me and we pulled out some more bodies and I can remember I was the last one to come

45

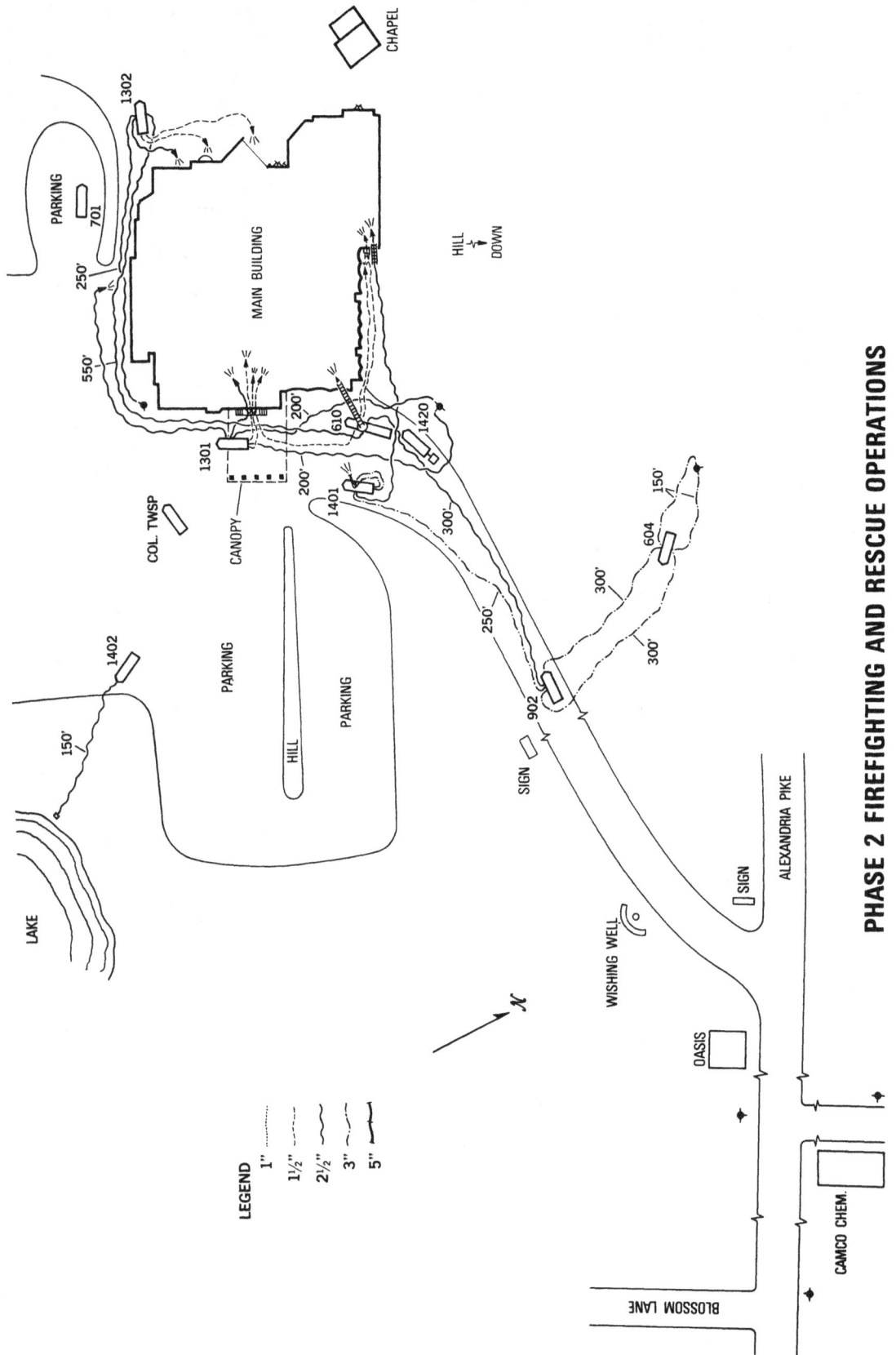

Figure 10.

THE BEVERLY HILLS SUPPER CLUB FIRE

The Garden Room area seen from the north of the Club from the garden area. Exit F is visible in the right center of the photo. (Credit: Mayhew Photographers)

out because I had gotten so damn tired that I couldn't even pull any. I was just in there pointing them out and knocking (stuff) out of the way, and saying, 'Get that one, get that one, get that one.' We never did get to the closet where they were stacked in the closet. And when I came out the door there was a Lieutenant...

... Well when I came out I thought that there was one more fireman left in there behind me. Because the last time I came out I saw the flame and the flame was coming which would have been from the west toward the east end. In other words the flames were coming from the Cabaret Room back toward the hallway, where we were at. Cause evidently it lapped over the top and it was starting to burn this way toward the hallway and these rooms where these bodies were and I can remember telling him I said, 'Is everybody out.' I said, 'Are you sure that nobody is left in there.' And he said, 'No,' and the doorway was burning. The flames just as I went out the door. Right above the doorway, the ceiling area there. That burst out into flame, flames burst out in the doorway and he had an inch and half hose and he turned that on at that time and it started putting them flames out and I had it. Well hell I couldn't breathe and I left and I went on out in front of the building, I sat down in the front of the building on a rock and I can remember talking to the Chief of the Covington Fire Department ... and I was having trouble breathing and (Ed) came up to me and he... said, '... The whole wall back there, the roof it is all burning,' he said that it looked like it was going to fall on the people that we drug (sic) out. So he said, 'Can you get somebody to get those people away from the wall?' And I walked back there again and there were 10 to 15 firemen standing around back there. And I said, 'Get them bodies and drag them down the hill,' and I guessed that they drug (sic) them down the hill maybe 30 or 35 yards down the hill and I went on down to my pumper, while I was on my way down that is when the wall collapsed on the outside on top of the hose lines...

Other arriving chiefs took charge of fire and rescue operations at the south, east, and west sides. Chief Riesenberg maintained command of fire operations at the front (south), and he sent additional personnel to the chapel exit as help arrived. (See Figure 10.)

When the Covington Fire Department arrived, they wanted to lay a 5-inch supply line up the driveway to 902, but traffic up and down the hill made them lay the 800 feet of 5-inch hose by hand. The supply line was fed

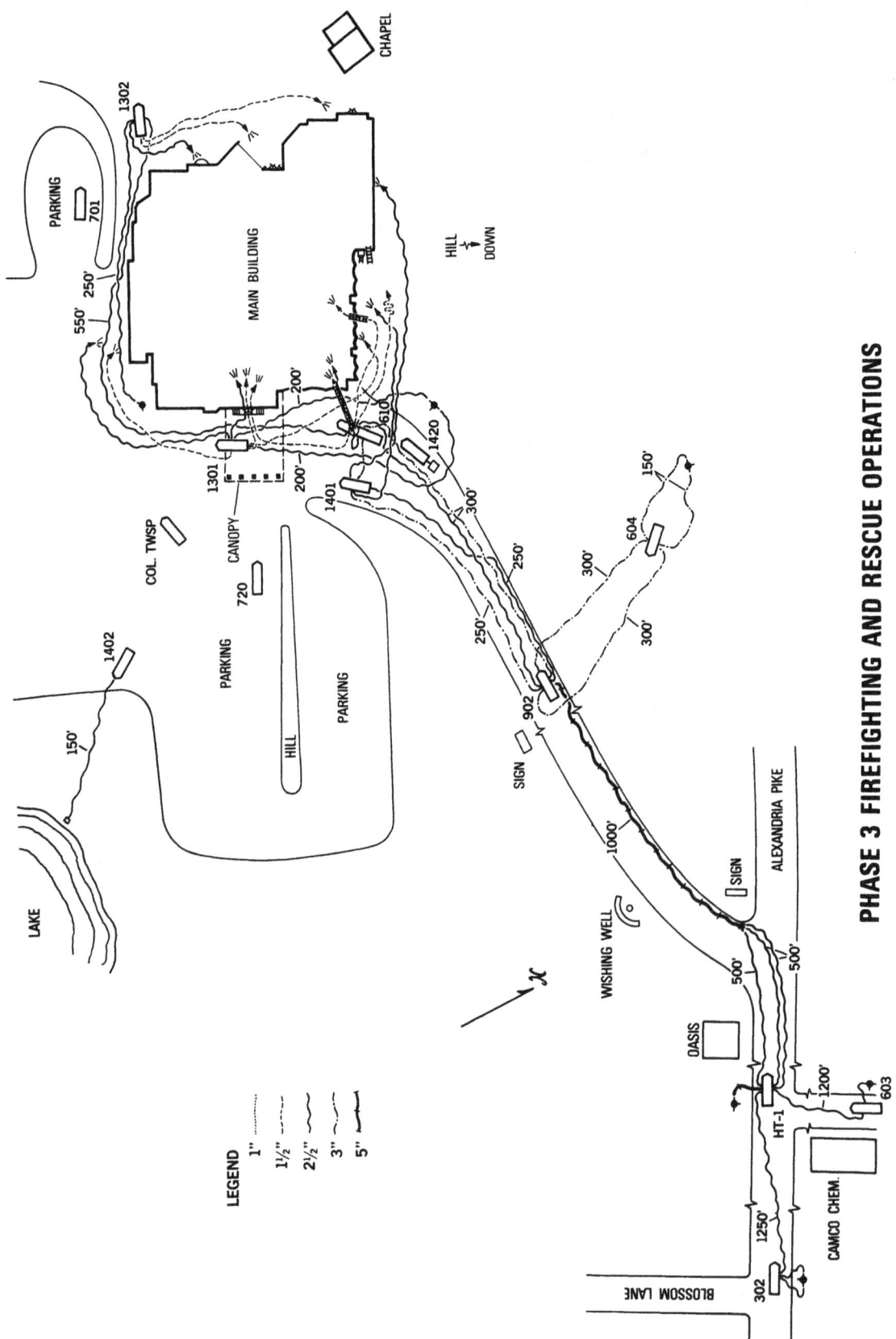

Figure 11.

by various engines on the highway, and at that point, 902 was being fed from two different relay sources. (See Figures 11 and 12.)

Sometime after Chief Riesenberg called for additional rescue squads, the previous Southgate fire chief arrived on the scene and asked Chief Riesenberg where he needed the most help. Chief Riesenberg told him that he needed extra ambulance and rescue units. The former chief said that he would handle the dispatching, and he apparently contacted the dispatcher. He may have contacted the county dispatcher because Kenton and Boone Counties (Kentucky), and Hamilton County (Ohio) responded with about thirty-four vehicles.

Half of the driveway to the Club was open for traffic, and Chief Riesenberg wanted to move another aerial unit up the driveway. He requested that ambulance drivers not use their sirens if they were transporting fatalities, and to use the sirens only if injured were being transported. The chief hoped that they might be able to hold back ambulances that were not carrying injured long enough to inch the aerial up the hill. However, the request was misinterpreted and all ambulances used their sirens whether they were carrying injured or dead. All efforts to move the second aerial up the driveway were abandoned.

At about 11:30 p.m., it had become apparent that the fire departments could do nothing inside, and fire fighters might be injured or killed. The decision to evacuate personnel from the building was made when the fire was completely out of control; the fire was not under control until approximately 2 a.m. The search for the remaining victims was begun at daylight the following morning, although the fire was not completely extinguished until Monday morning, May 30, 1977.

The Beverly Hills Supper Club fire involved every fire department in Campbell County. Each was represented either with personnel or equipment. Twenty-four fire departments sent ambulance or rescue units to the fire from Kenton, Boone, and Campbell Counties in Kentucky, and Hamilton County in Ohio. In all, approximately 522 fire fighters participated in the Beverly Hills Supper Club fire fighting and rescue operation.

VICTIMS OF THE FIRE

Before fire fighters arrived at the rear of the Club, some employees and patrons were pulling victims out of the Cabaret Room after the patrons had piled up at the double swinging doors leading to the service area near Exit A (chapel exit). Many of these victims — both patrons and employees — were still alive when they were dragged from the building. Doctors and nurses who had been attending a dinner in the Viennese Rooms tended to those who were still alive, and they were able to revive some occupants who did not show any life signs.

Fire fighters arrived at the rear of the Club at about 9:15 p.m.,* and continued the rescue operation. At the other exit on the south-east corner of the Cabaret Room (Exit B), the assistant chief from Newport dragged victims from the area behind the stage. (See "Fire Service and Rescue Operations" section.) Fire fighters continued rescue operations until the time they pulled out of the building because of the hazardous conditions; the fire burning throughout most of the building presented the danger of building collapse. One fire fighter reported: "We was ten foot at the very most inside. . . . the swinging doors — that's as far — I had two more people I coulda got a hold of (they were dead**). . . . they said pull out, we got outside. . ."

Cabaret Room victims in an area north of the Club, beyond the garden area. Garden Room area fire is in the background. Note that the victims have very minor burns — if any. (Credit: The Cincinnati Enquirer)

---

*The time is not confirmed, but is an estimated time based on fire fighter arrival time, sequence of fire fighter operations, and statements that employees were already rescuing victims from the Cabaret Room when fire fighters arrived at the rear of the building.

**Editorial note added by Southgate Fire Chief who reviewed transcript of interview.

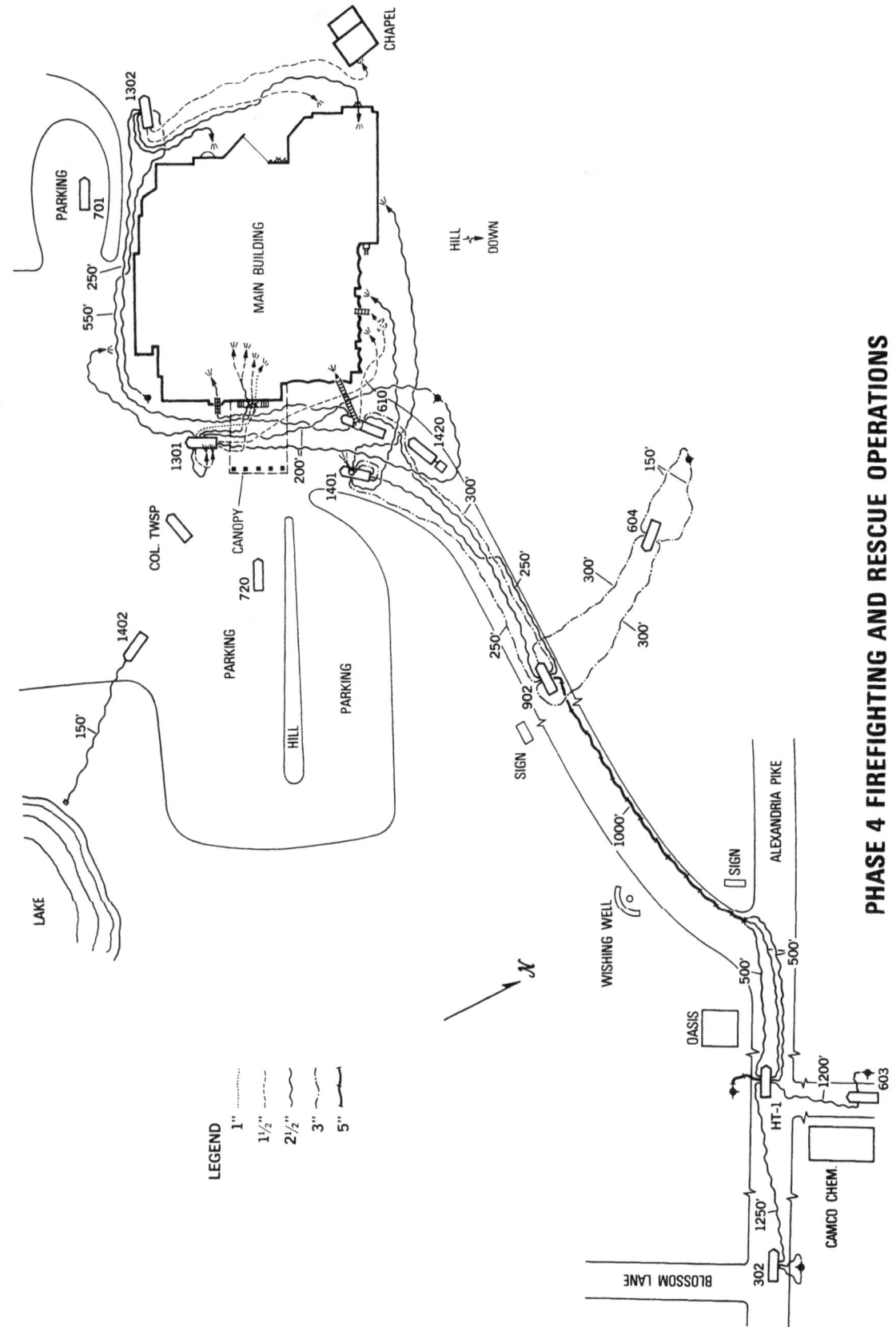

Figure 12.

THE BEVERLY HILLS SUPPER CLUB FIRE

A view of other Cabaret Room victims, looking north from the garden area. (Credit: Mayhew Photographers)

Victims pulled from the Cabaret Room had only minor burns — if any — and their clothing was not burned. After rescue operations ceased around 11:30 p.m., the fire continued to burn into the Cabaret Room and throughout the Club. The fire was not under control until 2:00 a.m. Sunday morning. Victims removed from the building after that time were severly burned.

Ninety-nine victims were taken out of the Cabaret Room on the night of the fire from Exit A. Most of these victims were inside the double swinging doors; some were in the service bar area; eleven were behind the bar; and one body was lying across the bar. Thirty-four victims were recovered from Exit B of the Cabaret Room. One was pulled out from behind the stage after a hole was battered through the wall. (See Figure 13.)

Fire fighters began the search for the remaining victims early Sunday morning after daylight. Fire fighters made their first sweep into the Cabaret Room at Exit A, and thirteen bodies were pulled out. Their next sweep was deeper, and they found eight bodies. Five bodies were recovered on the third sweep. At that point, fire fighters made a sweep that included the entire Cabaret Room, the entire hall, and part of the Empire Room. They found nothing on two sweeps. Three days later, two female victims were found on the roof of the Viennese Rooms with debris on top of them. Three* injured victims died later in the hospital. The total number of persons who died in the Beverly Hills Supper Club fire at the time of this report is 164.

The major cause of death in all the casualties was determined to be smoke inhalation and acute carbon monoxide intoxication. Some of the fatally injured managed to escape the building, only to collapse and die outside the building. A few others died at local hospitals. The exact number of injured was not determined due to the fact that local hospitals suspended their normal out-patient treatment procedures because of the severity of the Beverly Hills Supper Club emergency. Approximately seventy occupants of the Club were known to be injured, but the actual number of injured is considered to be higher.

Not all occupants who died in the Cabaret Room were from the Cabaret Room or in the Cabaret Room just prior to the fire. At least two of the victims were from the Empire Room, and it is believed that other patrons may have mistakenly entered the Cabaret Room in their attempt to escape from the building.

Of the 164 fatalities at the Beverly Hills Supper Club, 161 died during the initial fire incident and three others died at a local hospital. Sixty-six of the 161 were male and ninety-five were female. Thirty-four of the 161 victims were severely burned, and 127 were not. Of the three victims who died at the hospital, two were male and one was a female.

An armory was used as a temporary morgue on the night of the fire, and at about 2:00 a.m. the following morning, the fatalities were being transported to the armory, where they were examined by identification teams. By 4:00 a.m., 127 bodies had been transported.

The first badly burned victims were taken to the armory beginning at 11:00 a.m. Sunday morning, with the

---

*The total number of fatalities is based on information provided by the Southgate Fire Chief: that 134 victims were recovered from the building on the night of the fire, that twenty-eight severly burned bodies were recovered after the fire was under control, and that two fatalities occurred in a local hospital. The Coroner's report states that 127 victims of the fire were recovered from the Club during the night of the fire and that the badly burned bodies recovered later totaled thirty-four. The Coroner reported that three victims died in local hospitals.

Table 2.2 Blood Analysis Results

	Victim One	Victim Two	Victim Three	Victim Four	Victim Five
Carbon monoxide (percent of saturation)	39%	60%	42%	22%	54%
Ethyl alcohol (percent by weight)	0.05%	0.06%	0.03%	0.10%	Negative
Cyanide	Negative	Negative	Insufficient sample	Insufficient sample	Negative
Chlorinated hydrocarbons	Negative	Negative	Negative	Negative	Negative

last group transported at 2:00 p.m. Two more severely burned fatalities were located on June 1, 1977, bringing the total number of victims to 161.

Identification of many of the victims was difficult, but all 161 persons were identified by June 9. Thirty-seven bodies were identified through dental records, fifteen by autopsy, and six victims were identified by finger prints.

Autopsies were performed on a very limited number of the bodies. Only five autopsy reports were available to the NFPA through the Kentucky State Police. All five reports state that the cause of death was from smoke inhalation, with acute carbon monoxide intoxication and either subtotal or extensive body incineration.

Blood samples of the five victims were examined for carbon monoxide, ethyl alcohol, cyanide and chlorinated hydrocarbons. (See Table 2.2.)

The coroner's final opinion was that all of the 161 victims (excluding the three hospital fatalities) died of smoke inhalation and carbon monoxide intoxication, with no other poisonous substances found.

DAMAGE TO THE BUILDING

The Beverly Hills Supper Club was completely destroyed in the May 28, 1977 fire. Roof collapse involved all portions of the building except along the

General damage view in the area of the Empire Room. The view is to the front, or south end of the Club. The second floor Crystal Room is visible in the upper right of the photo. At the time the photo was taken, the search for victims was still in progress. (Credit: NFPA)

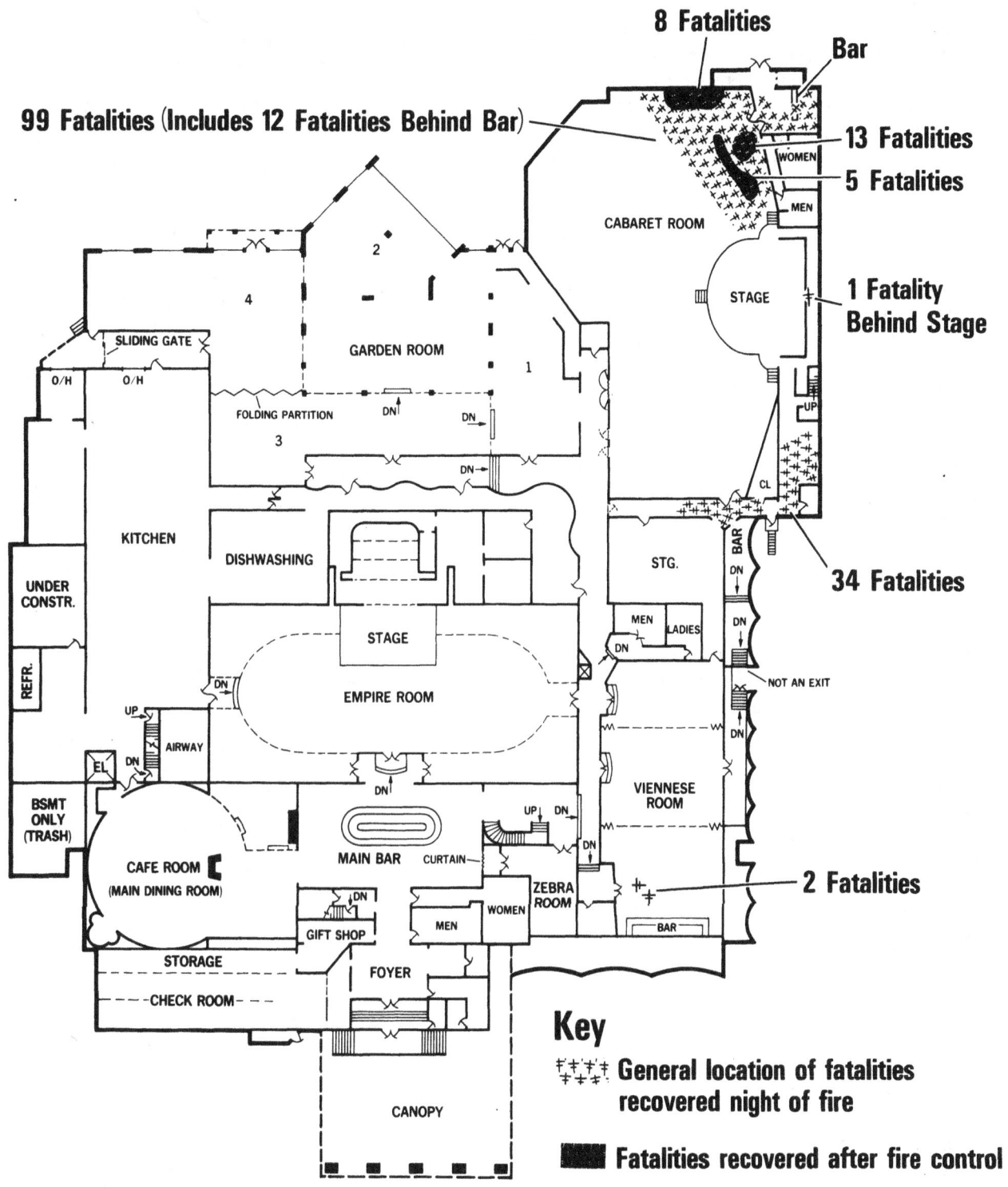

FATALITIES

Figure 13.

outside west wall of the kitchen and the extreme front or south end of the building, which was the front entrance and foyer. The areas without roof collapse were damaged by smoke and heat. The basement was not heavily damaged, except where steel beams and columns collapsed in two areas, allowing the floor above to partially collapse into the basement.

Areas where destruction was complete and where there was roof collapse were the Cabaret, Garden, Empire, Viennese, Cafe dining, and check rooms, most of the Crystal Rooms (second floor), and the main bar and Zebra Room.

The coatroom portion of the building and the second floor toilet area and roof over the Zebra Room were completely burned. Only the bottom portions of internal partition wood studs and some outside wall framing remained in the coatroom.

In the process of searching for victims during the two weeks following the fire, all of the collapsed roof, walls, and debris east of the kitchen and north of the main bar was cleared. This left only a clean, concrete floor slab.

SURVIVORS' ACTIONS AND REACTIONS

Employee and patron actions during the fire and reactions to the fire have been previously described, and will be discussed in greater detail in the "Human Behavior" discussion in Section III, "Analysis of the Fire." In general, most employees in the Club responded to notification of the fire by returning to their areas of responsibility and evacuating customers. However, some employees did not believe the fire was serious and continued to serve their customers; others tried to determine how serious the fire was.

Most patrons at the Beverly Hills Supper Club exited from the building when they were notified of the fire. However, some patrons did not believe the person who made the announcement of the fire, and some did not react to the notice because they did not think the danger was great. Some patrons reported that they were told to stay low or to keep their heads down, but many did not follow these instructions because they were afraid that they would be pushed down if they did so. One patron indicated she was crowded so closely with other patrons during the exit from the building that it was impossible for her to bend over to stay below the smoke.

Actions and reactions on the part of both employees and patrons were varied. The following excerpts depict some particularly unusual actions. These excerpts are given here only to record reactions to the Beverly Hills Supper Club fire situation; no attempt will be made to explain or analyze these actions.

Hostess in the main bar:

- .... I saw her open the Zebra doors and I saw some smoke come out and she closed them and I let it pass me. I honestly do not know why but I think because I had all these customers on my mind that I had to be seated for dinner so I took some people in the dining room and I came out and (Nancy) said, '(Barbara), I have to call the fire department.' She said, 'We have a small fire.' I said, 'Okay,' and course (sic) she proceeded, you know, I saw her start to dial the phone and I knew what customers I had to seat because they were at the bar and they were ready for their table and I took them into the dining room and I stood there and talked to them for just a few minutes. I came back out and (Nancy) said, '(Barbara),' she said, 'get out of here,' she said, 'this building is on fire,' and I just stood there for a few minutes, you know and I looked down the mirrored hallway, which is near the Zebra Room, you know, and I could see the smoke coming this way. . . .

Hostess directly outside the Garden Rooms:

- One of the waiters went running by and the other hostess came up to me and said, 'There is a fire in the building,' but to wait a minute because she didn't know how much it was and then the waiter ran back by and I said, 'Are you serious?' and he said, 'Yes'. . . .

  . . . . I didn't even check Garden 1 or Garden 4 when the parties were going on. I was just thinking of the people I had seated and everything for dinner. And I got them all out and all those rooms were empty. . . .

Model in a second-floor dressing room:

- . . . . We sat in a room trying to wait until all of the other guests were finished eating and someone was supposed to keep us posted, you know, how far along they were with their meal before we could get dressed. We were sitting there and it was getting rather late, I guess it was a little after nine and one of the girls sent one out to check to see how far

> along the other people were eating and she came back in and she said there was a small cigarette fire, I don't know who informed her, but she opened the door and a little smoke came in not much. A small cigarette fire, but they said it was under control. So she closed the door back and we had like a separate air conditioning unit in there so the air was clear but you know she closed it and you could smell the smoke and so we sat back down. . . .
>
> . . . . All I could hear them saying was, 'Keep low,' well when I tried to crouch a little bit I was afraid that I would get pushed down, so I just remained standing, because there were too many people trying to rush out.

Bartender, in hallway, who had been working the Empire Room:

- > . . . . My first instinct was to go back to the Empire Room. So, that's where I went.

Patron in Cabaret Room:

- > . . . . I'd say maybe at the time he (the busboy) said there was a small fire in the building, only 30 or 40 percent of the people started to move at that time. The people down in the pits next to the stage weren't moving at all. They seemed to be satisfied to just sit right where they were. As we were going down the aisle, back toward the exit of the Cabaret Room, one man remarked, 'I don't know why everybody is in such a panic.' He was still sitting there. His wife was up. She looked petrified. This guy was just sitting there. He didn't appear to be intoxicated to the point where he didn't know what was going on. He was just one of these guys that sort of shows off. He said, 'If we go, we go.' I went on by, that's the last I heard him say.

Patron exiting through the main bar:

- > . . . . I just recall people — people saying, 'Don't panic, stay calm.' People up front saying, 'Stay as low as you can.' I don't know how many possibly can tell (sic) there was behind us because there was one time I did glance back, there was a bigger man that was yelling the same thing. 'Keep calm, we have got it made now, we got it made now.' I saw the light at that time. I knew that if nobody stumbled or fell over it (sic) we could hold our breath that long.

Patrons in Garden Room:

Patron 1: *. . . . She said, 'I opened the doors to the Zebra Room and it was full of smoke.' By her frantic attitude I feel that she must have been the person that noticed it first. She was just about a basket case, she was able to walk but she was crying and very distressed.*

Patron 2: *With her expressions there wasn't a soul in that room that hesitated to go out.*

Questioner: *Nobody doubted her at all?*

Patron 2: *No. There was no . . . when she said for everybody to get out there was another table that was sitting alongside us closer to the window with about 32 people I think and they got right up and got out right away. I mean nobody hesitated a minute about getting out. There were . . . cause everybody could tell from her expressions that she meant business.*

RECONSTRUCTION OF A TRAGEDY

(Copyright © 1977, *The Courier-Journal.* Reprinted with permission.)

The Beverly Hills Supper Club Fire

Section III

ANALYSIS OF THE FIRE

ORIGIN, CAUSE, DEVELOPMENT, AND SPREAD

Origin and Cause of Fire

Based on a thorough examination of physical evidence and information available through interviews of occupants and employees of the Beverly Hills Supper Club, the investigation team concluded that the fire originated in a concealed space within the Zebra Room. The most probable source of ignition was electrical in nature.

The precise electrical equipment (lighting fixture, switch, receptacle, outlet, or fixed wiring), or the form of heat of ignition (short circuit arc, arc from faulty contact, or heat from electrical fixture), could not be determined during two weeks of intensive investigation by the investigation team following the fire.

Early reports of fire cause immediately following the fire, and various other reports of fire cause and area of origin, required that the investigation team consider and examine dozens of theories. Reports that the fire was caused by a transformer explosion, that the fire started in the kitchen, or that the fire originated in the basement were explored and then ruled out. There was no evidence of a transformer explosion and positively no indication that the fire originated in the kitchen area. However, the theory that the fire originated in the basement was reasonable, and was therefore given much attention and consideration. There was evidence of fire in the basement under the main bar area, and there were small-diameter holes through the concrete floor of the first floor (directly above the basement area), such as conduit and pipe openings. The strongest evidence disproving the theory that the fire originated in the basement was the testimony of employees who had traveled through the basement area after the fire was discovered on the first floor. Their reports that they did not smell smoke and did not see smoke or fire ruled out the theory that the fire originated in the basement.

In addition, examination of the floor openings in relation to the fire location in the basement and the Zebra Room on the first floor did not support the basement theory.

The determination of fire cause was hampered by the degree of destruction of the building (see "Damage to the Building," Section II). The north, south, and west walls of the Zebra Room alcove, where the reservationist was located, were nearly completely destroyed. A steel column in the basement supporting this area had partially collapsed, causing floors to pitch downward and resulting in cracks and openings in the floor slab that did not exist prior to the fire.

Testimony of employees and patrons, however, was consistent in placing the fire in the Zebra Room at the time of discovery. Numerous and consistent items of information in the transcripts led to the conclusion that the fire originated either in a concealed space within the walls of the Zebra Room or between suspended ceilings above the Zebra Room, and that the fire smoldered or burned for a considerable period of time before breaking through either the ceiling or the walls into the room itself.

The only possible source of ignition that could be located within the concealed spaces was electrical in nature. By reconstructing what was left of the ceiling support system in the Zebra Room and the bar joists that supported the floor above, it was determined that

The north wall of the Zebra Room, which shows wall finish in the lower left corner. The door opening to the Hallway of the Mirrors is visible. (Credit: NFPA)

combustible ceiling tile was adhered to the wire lath and plaster ceiling in the Zebra Room. Fixtures believed to have been mounted in the Zebra Room were recessed 10½ inches into the ceiling. One of these had an upper portion (approximately 4 inches by 4 inches) melted away, indicating an extremely high degree of heat in this area. It was the opinion of electrical specialist members of the investigation team that the short circuiting or arcing of electrical wires did not cause the melting of such a large area. The heat from the recessed ceiling lights was considered a strong possible ignition source, but the clearance between the top of the light fixture and the combustible tile was too great to make this more than a speculative theory. Another possibility was that the tiles had fallen from the ceiling after a period of time and had come in contact with the lighting fixtures.

Because the roof leaked in the area over the Crystal and Zebra Rooms, it was considered that the moisture could possibly have caused a breakdown of the asbestos insulation of the light fixture wiring, and that the bare wiring came in contact with combustible ceiling tiles or other combustible materials. No positive evidence, however, could be found to support this theory.

A private investigation team theorized that the wiring to the pump motor in the pool under the curved stairway was the ignition source. This theory presented a logical electrical ignition source that was in the concealed space between the Zebra Room and the pool enclosure, and therefore was carefully examined. The water pump was still submerged in water after the fire. The rubber cord from the pump was enclosed in plastic tubing, which passed through a retaining fiberglass wall. At this point a hole was cut (approximately ⅝-inch in diameter) in a surrounding sheet metal line through which the cord was passed. Pictures were taken showing a taped section (which at first appeared to be a splice) of the cord where it passed through the hole.

At first it was determined that the 6-foot cord that was attached to the pump motor was spliced and taped to extend the cord to reach a duplex receptacle in the area that was used for a cord-equipped decorative fountain light cord only. Statements during interrogations revealed that the pump cord continued through a wire lath and plaster wall, which was covered on the Zebra side with a wood paneling, and was plugged into a wall receptacle within the Zebra Room. The close scrutiny of several investigators disclosed that the tape was meant to be a bushing or protective means to pass the cord through the sheet metal wall, that it was not short circuited at this point, and that the mark on the cord could conceivably have been caused by the heat of the fire upon the sheet metal.

Therefore, it was the opinion of members of the investigation team that the water pump and/or its cord did not cause the fire, based on the following facts:

• A test of the pump, performed on-site, proved

THE BEVERLY HILLS SUPPER CLUB FIRE

The north wall of the small corridor (Hallway of the Mirrors) outside the Zebra Room, where the curved stairs were located. Note the wall and ceiling construction. (Credit: NFPA)

that it was totally free of any defects and in excellent running condition.

- The heat of the fire upon the sheet metal wall melted and shaped the cord to the hole location. However, the cord was not shorted, i.e., the copper stranded conductors were still insulated. There were no arcing or sparking marks on either sheet metal or the wire lath.

- As indicated, if the cord had been plugged into a receptacle in the Zebra Room and the point of fire origin had been at this receptacle, it would have been detected by the people who investigated the smell of smoke.

- A chandelier type of wall fixture mounted on this wall did not effectively seal off the partition, as it was attached to the wall with wood screws and merely wired to an open device box. It would have admitted any smoke in the partition into the room and, again, would have been detected by those who checked on the smell of smoke. (NOTE: The method of mounting and wiring of the wall fixtures was indicated by several other identical fixtures in the Zebra Room.)

- The over-current protective devices were circuit breakers, and would automatically trip on short-circuit conditions.

It is to be noted also that after the cord passed through the wall, it was broken off, as were other wiring methods (electrical metallic tubing) in the immediate area, which would have been caused by falling or collapsing debris (or the removal of debris).

The final determination by the investigation team was that the Beverly Hills Supper Club fire originated in a concealed space within the Zebra Room and that the most probable cause of ignition within this area was electrical in nature. However, the specific form of heat of ignition, the circumstances, and the exact location could not be determined.

Fire Development

The spread of the fire from the Zebra Room to other areas of the building can be traced through the various accounts of employees, patrons, and fire fighters, as documented in the transcripts of interviews. Exact times that the fire sequence occurred could not be identified in an initial study of a sample of the transcript information, but the information appears to be adequate to allow a detailed study of all transcripts and questionnaires that would accurately establish the time of fire discovery, the times that various rooms became untenable, and the time when smoke and flame entered the Cabaret Room.

It was estimated that initially the fire was confined to the Zebra Room for several minutes as employees notified the management, located fire extinguishers, and attempted to fight the fire. The time of fire discovery was approximately 8:45 p.m. to 8:50 p.m. Thick, black smoke spread into the main bar area, into the immediate area around the Hallway of the Mirrors, and up the curved stairs to the Crystal Rooms. The smoke filled the front of the building, including the Cafe dining room and the front foyer. Smoke and flame apparently did not travel beyond the older, front, two-story section of the building until the dense black smoke, followed by flame, traveled rapidly northward along the main north-south corridor and entered the Garden Rooms and the Cabaret Room. Flames were then shooting out the rear doors in the Garden Rooms area. The time was about 9:05 to 9:10 when the smoke, gases, heat, and flames entered the Cabaret Room.

The main body of the fire then spread steadily from the front of the Club into the center of the building. At some point after the occupants in the Cabaret Room had been overcome by the initial wave of smoke, flame, and heat, the fire vented itself through the roof of the building somewhere in the area east of the Empire Room. The smoke level throughout the building lifted at that time and allowed fire fighters and rescue workers to enter the Cabaret Room with less difficulty. The fire then continued to spread throughout all areas of the Beverly Hills Supper Club except along the west side (kitchen area) and the basement.

Although fire did not enter the kitchen area per se, heat from the fire caused the suspended ceiling in the kitchen to partially collapse. Melted glassware along the east side of the kitchen nearest to the center of the building would indicate that temperatures in the kitchen were 1400°F or higher[5] at the height of the fire.

Fire Spread to the Cabaret Room [6]

The presence of combustible ceiling tile and wood materials within the ceiling space of the Zebra Room provided a fuel supply for the continued spread of the fire through the concealed space of fire origin and other concealed spaces. There was an intense heat build-up within the concealed space that ultimately resulted in the accumulation of smoke and hot gases within the Zebra Room itself. The fire was apparently discovered at this point, and attempts were made to extinguish it. During the time these attempts were being made, flames erupted through the doorway of the Zebra Room into the Hallway of the Mirrors, which knocked employees who were attempting to fight the fire away from the door opening. The fire within the Zebra Room continued to build until it broke out of the room through the double doors located at the north end of the room.

It is theorized that flashover occurred in the Zebra Room (simultaneous ignition of all combustible materials within the room), and the room resembled a furnace because of the simultaneous burning of room furnishings. These furnishings included several wood tables, about twenty-three chairs (see Appendix C for details on the chairs), and the carpet. Under these circumstances, the walls of the room, which were covered with $\frac{3}{16}$-inch combustible hardboard paneling, would also have been burning and contributing to the fire. Richard G. Bright, in his report, *Beverly Hills Supper Club Fire, Southgate, Kentucky, May 28, 1977 — An Analysis of the Development and Spread of Fire from the Room of Fire Origin (Zebra Room) to the Cabaret Room,* suggests a probable scenario for the action of the fire:[7]

"This furnace-like fire had only one immediate flue or vent available to it and this was the pair of doors at the north end of the room. From eye-witness accounts, apparently one door, the west leaf, was partially open, perhaps at 45 degrees or so (confirmed by on-site evidence). It was likely the other leaf was open also, and the physical evidence suggested that it may have been fully open. Regardless of whether this leaf was open, partially open, or closed, this would have been of significance only through the first minutes of the fire as the fire's intensity was of such magnitude that the fire would have quickly consumed the top part of this wooden door.

"The venting of the fire through this doorway resulted in the passage of smoke, flames and heat through the upper part of the doorway at relatively high velocities, with an inrush of cold, fresh air, at lower velocities, near the floor. As the smoke, flames and hot gases left the Zebra Room they were propelled across the ceiling of the small corridor directly outside the Zebra Room until they hit the far wall, some 20 feet distant. Here, the flames and hot gases split, with part of flames and hot gases turning down and part turning sideways in both direction. The thin, plywood paneling, on the far wall of the small corridor, would have ignited readily under the impact of this flame and hot gas exposure.

"In the meantime, the fire on the carpet in the Zebra Room would have spread through the doorway also, slower than the flames and hot gases along the ceiling, but sustained by the thermal radiation down onto the carpet by the smoke and hot gas layer at the ceiling. In examination of the Zebra Room, it was found that the carpet and its padding were completely consumed, down to bare concrete, in the doorway opening, the only location in the Zebra Room with such extensive damage.

"The flames and hot gases leaving the Zebra Room, in addition to impinging on the plywood paneling of the small corridor wall, also were probably passing up the stairway to the west of the lobby, into the main bar to the west, and through the 15-foot opening into the main corridor to the east.

"It was apparent, from the on-site investigation, that sufficient heat was present in the stream of hot gases passing through this 15-foot opening into the main corridor to ignite combustibles present in this corridor. These combustibles consisted of the hardboard paneling on the walls and the carpet systems on the floor.

"As the flames and hot gases entered the main corridor, the carpet and the hardboard paneling began to contribute combustible gases to the fire through the driving off of the combustible volatiles in the carpet and the paneling. This resulted in the extension of the burning down the corridor. At about this period in time, sufficient thermal radiation was being directed down on the carpet surface from the smoke and hot gas layer at the ceiling to cause the spread of the fire on the carpet from the small corridor through the 15-foot doorway, into the main corridor. Once this happened, the fire in the corridor was very nearly a self-sustaining fire, feeding on both the carpet and the paneling, with each contributing to the growth and spread of the other. Even so, energy was still being supplied into the main corridor from the fire in the Zebra Room and the small corridor outside. From this point, fire spread rapidly down the main corridor, with visible fire rolling along underneath the ceiling and a secondary fire travelling along on the carpet face, trailing behind the ceiling fire."

Analysis of Fire Development and Spread[8]

The Zebra Room had two sets of double doors, of wood construction, that opened and closed by swinging into the room. One set was to the west, opening into the reservationist's alcove. This west opening allowed the fire to pass into the main bar area at a later stage in the fire sequence; in the early stages of the fire, the reservationist recalls that these doors were closed. The other doorway, to the north, opened into a small, east-west corridor approximately 32 feet long and 20 feet wide. This small corridor opened into the main bar on the west, and into the main north-south corridor (to the Cabaret Room) on the east through a 15-foot wide opening. A curved, steel stairway to the second floor was located in this small corridor just to the left (west) of the Zebra Room's north doors and against the north wall of the Zebra Room.

The ceiling of this small corridor was of concealed, kerf and spline, mineral-type, acoustical tile. Due to its mineral nature, this tile is likely to have a very low flame spread index and can be considered to be noncombustible. The walls of this small corridor were covered with a decoratively finished plywood paneling, somewhere between $3/16$-inch and $1/4$-inch thick, applied over wood furring strips.* This plywood was combustible, and although samples were not available to establish a flame spread index, it was probably between 100 and 200, based on ASTM E-84 testing procedures and National Bureau of Standards' knowledge of the behavior of these materials.

The floor of the small corridor was covered by a carpet installed over an underlayment (padding). The carpet was the same as used in the Zebra Room, according to the Kentucky State Crime Laboratory. Analysis of the Zebra Room carpet by the National Bureau of Standards (NBS) indicates it was a nylon carpet with a low pile height (0.375 inches) and dense construction (58 oz/yd^2). The padding has not been identified, but was most likely of heavy, commercial grade, as this was characteristic of underlayments recovered from other portions of the Club.

The main north-south corridor, leading north from the 15-foot wide opening within the east portion of the Club to the Cabaret Room, was approximately 8 feet wide and about 150 feet long. In addition to serving doorways to the Viennese Rooms on the east and the Empire Room on the west, this corridor connected to two cross corridors — one to the east along the south wall of the Cabaret Room, and one to the west between the Garden Rooms and the employees' crossover service corridor. This main corridor terminated outside of the principal entrance to the Cabaret Room.

The main corridor's ceiling was of concealed, kerf and spline, mineral-type, acoustical tile — essentially *noncombustible in nature*. The floor was covered with a carpet applied over an underlayment. Based on NBS Analysis, the carpet was essentially of woven, wool construction with a small amount (less than 10 percent) of acrylic fibers blended in. The pile height was 0.25 inches and weight was 78 oz/yd^2. The underlayment was identified by NBS to be jute with a pad height of 0.5 inches and a weight of 51 oz/yd^2.

The corridor walls were covered with a decoratively finished, hardboard paneling applied over wood furring strips. This paneling was combustible, and although its flame spread index could not be determined, experience at the National Bureau of Standards indicates that it probably ranged somewhere between 150 and 200. This paneling was applied to both walls of the corridor for its full length except for the curvi-

---
*The small pieces of paneling remaining in this corridor were swollen and/or delaminated, making accurate measurements difficult.

A view of Exit B from the Cabaret Room. Note that the steps from the platform to the ground are mostly burned away. The debris on the left was the roof between the facade and the building. (Note: This is the exit referred to by the assistant chief who dragged victims from behind the dressing room area — southeast corner — of the Cabaret Room.) (Credit: NFPA)

linear wall at the west cross corridor, which was of exposed brick, and another section of the corridor near the Cabaret Room, which was paneled on one side with interior doors placed side by side.

Effects of Smoke[9]

Based on NBS experience on corridor fires, the smoke from the original fire in the Zebra Room and from the fire in the corridors would have spread in the same direction as the fire, but at an earlier period in this sequence. In other words, the smoke would have reached the Cabaret Room some time ahead of the fire. This smoke would have appeared to be dark — almost black — to the occupants. In addition, it would have been extremely irritating, causing tearing of the eyes and a burning sensation to the nose. This was due to the nature of the materials undergoing combustion, i.e., the carpets and wall paneling. In addition, for a fire of this type, the smoke would have contained certain toxic gas species, with carbon monoxide as the principal gas. Carbon monoxide, although colorless and odorless in the quantities likely to have been present in the early stages of this fire, induces confusion and disorientation in the person who inhales it. As the levels of the gas increased in the later stages of the fire, carbon monoxide resulted in unconsciousness and ultimate death to many of the occupants.

Effects of Air Conditioning[10]

The public spaces of the Beverly Hills Supper Club were completely air conditioned, and the system was in operation at the time of the fire. There was no central system, but a series of separate systems servicing various areas. It is not clear whether the air conditioning systems had any adverse effects during the fire, such as spreading or retarding the movement of smoke or of the fire, during the early stages. Once the fire left the Zebra Room, however, it is apparent that the fire was probably of sufficient energy to overpower the air handling system. Some newspaper accounts suggested that the air conditioning system helped to spread the smoke and the fire. This hypothesis may or may not be true, but the smoke and the fire would have had no difficulty spreading throughout the Club and through the public use spaces, such as the corridors, as there were no barriers to the movement of smoke and fire through these spaces, and the fire had sufficient thermal energy to move the smoke through these spaces.

Rapidity of Fire Spread[11]

The rapidity of the spread of fire from the Zebra Room to the Cabaret Room, via the main corridor, undoubtedly was a factor in the large loss of life in the Cabaret Room. While it is not possible to give more than an educated estimate, it is postulated that once the fire had emerged from the Zebra Room and crossed over the main corridor, the fire probably reached the Cabaret Room between two to five minutes later.

Conclusions From Flame Spread Analysis[12]

• Once the Zebra Room was fully involved in fire, i.e., flashover had occurred, sufficient thermal energy was available to push the fire out of the north double doors into the small corridor outside.

• Sufficient thermal energy was available from the Zebra Room to ignite and sustain a fire in this small corridor on the carpet and plywood wall paneling.

• The combination of the thermal energy outputs of the Zebra Room and small corridor were of sufficient magnitude to ignite and sustain a fire in the main corridor to the Cabaret Room.

- Once the fire was established in the main corridor, the fire progressed rapidly towards the Cabaret Room, probably reaching the Cabaret Room between two to five minutes after entering the main corridor.

- The fire in the main corridor ultimately blocked the west exits from the Cabaret Room, leaving the remaining occupants with only Exits A and B.

- The air conditioning system does not appear to have played any significant role in the spread of fire towards the Cabaret Room.

LIFE SAFETY CODE ANALYSIS

The analysis and conclusions in this section are primarily based on the application of the 1976 *Life Safety Code*.[13] This report does not include an analysis of the Beverly Hills Supper Club fire in terms of other Codes (except where otherwise noted) that may have been applicable.

The 1976 edition of the *Life Safety Code* was used for this analysis so that the conditions at the Beverly Hills Supper Club on the date of the fire could be compared to the latest edition of the *Life Safety Code*. It is recognized that the 1976 edition of the *Life Safety Code* was not in effect in Kentucky at any time during construction phases or operation of the Beverly Hills Supper Club.

The *Life Safety Code* deals with life safety from fire and like emergencies. It covers construction, protection, and occupancy features to minimize danger to life from fire, smoke, fumes, or panic before buildings are vacated; and it specifies the number, size, and arrangement of exit facilities sufficient to permit prompt escape of occupants from buildings in case of fire. The *Code* recognizes that life safety is more than a matter of exits; accordingly, it deals with various matters besides exits that are considered essential to life safety. The *Code* does not attempt to cover general fire prevention or building construction features, such as are commonly dealt with in fire prevention codes and building codes.

Fundamental Requirements

Fundamental requirements of the *Life Safety Code* stipulate that:

- Every building shall have sufficient exits to permit the prompt escape of occupants in case of fire.

- Every building shall be provided with exits of kinds, numbers, location, and appropriate capacity to afford all occupants convenient facilities for escape.

- Every exit shall be clearly visible or the route to reach it shall be conspicuously indicated, and each path of escape shall be so arranged or marked, in its entirety, that the way to a place of safety is unmistakable.

- Every vertical way of exit shall be suitably enclosed or protected to afford reasonable safety to occupants while using exits.

Another fundamental requirement addresses the necessity of maintaining free and unobstructed egress from all parts of a building when it is occupied, and specifically states that no lock or fastening shall be installed to prevent free escape from the inside of any building.*

The following discussion of various sections of the *Life Safety Code*, dealing with means of egress, requirements for places of assembly, and other appropriate sections of the *Code*, will relate directly to many of these fundamental requirements. The items considered in this analysis, for the most part, concern specific requirements of the *Code*, but it should be noted that many of the fundamental requirements of the *Life Safety Code* will also be discussed.

Classification of Occupancy

The Beverly Hills Supper Club was classified as a place of assembly in NFPA 101, *Code for Safety to Life from Fire in Buildings and Structures*, 1976 Edition.

Occupant Load**

From the information provided by interviews, on-site inspection, and building drawings, the Beverly Hills Supper Club was classified as a Class A place of assembly, which means that it had a capacity of 1,000 persons or more (8-1.3.1).***

The *Life Safety Code* specifies the types of building construction permitted for places of assembly. The Beverly Hills Supper Club was constructed essentially of unprotected, noncombustible construction. This construction type is not permitted for Class A places of assembly by the *Life Safety Code*. Class A places of assembly are permitted by the *Code* on any level of a building of fire-resistive construction and (except for theaters or dance halls) on the level of exit discharge of

---

*An exception to this requirement allows locks in occupancies such as correctional institutions, where supervisory personnel are continually on duty and effective provisions are made to remove occupants in case of fire.

**Occupant load is defined in the *Life Safety Code* as the total number of persons that may occupy a building or portion thereof at any one time.

***References to specific sections of the *Life Safety Code* will be included in the text of these discussions, in parentheses.

Table 3.1 Net Floor Area and Occupant Load For Rooms at the Beverly Hills Supper Club

Room	Net floor area	Occupant load
Cabaret Room @ 15 sq ft	7,669 sq ft	511
Garden Rooms @ 15 sq ft	9,536 sq ft	636
Empire Room @ 15 sq ft	6,798 sq ft	447
Viennese Rooms @ 15 sq ft	3,840 sq ft	256
Cafe dining room, bar, foyer, and Zebra Room @ 15 sq ft	7,210 sq ft	481
@ 3 sq ft	425 sq ft	142
Crystal Rooms @ 15 sq ft	3,928 sq ft	262
		2,375 Total

buildings of heavy timber, protected noncombustible, protected ordinary, or protected wood-frame construction. In buildings of unprotected construction, only a Class C place of assembly is permitted, and then only at the level of exit discharge. (A Class C place of assembly is one with a capacity of 300 persons or less.)

The minimum occupant load for which exits must be provided as required by the *Life Safety Code* in any assembly building, structure, or portion thereof is determined by dividing the net floor area or space assigned to that use by the square feet per occupant. Square feet per occupant is based on 3 square feet per person for standing room or waiting space, 7 square feet per person for concentrated use without fixed seats, and 15 square feet per person for an assembly area of less concentrated use, such as a dining room, drinking establishment, or lounge.

Based on the net floor area divided by the appropriate number of square feet, it was determined that the total occupant load at the Beverly Hills Supper Club was 2,375 persons. The occupant load for rooms or groups of rooms is shown in Table 3.1.

Means of Egress Requirements

The *Life Safety Code* requires that every building or structure — new or old — designed for human occupancy shall be provided with exits sufficient to allow the prompt escape of occupants in the event of fire or other emergency (2-1). The Beverly Hills Supper Club was not provided with exits sufficient to permit the prompt escape of occupants in case of fire. Every place of assembly and every individual room used as a place of assembly shall have exits sufficient to provide for the total capacity (occupant load) and these shall be as follows:

• No individual unit of exit width shall serve more than 100 persons.

• Doors leading outside the building at grade level, or not more than three risers above or below grade, shall serve no more than 100 persons per exit unit.

• Stairs or other type of exit not specified above, shall serve no more than 75 persons per exit unit.

The total number of exit units required for the Beverly Hills Supper Club, based on 100 persons per unit of exit width (doors at grade level) and considering the occupant load based on square footage as previously determined, is 27.5 exit units. The number of exit units required, however, would actually be greater than this, considering that the *Life Safety Code* requires a main exit that will accommodate one-half of the total occupant load, and requires other exits to be of sufficient width to accommodate two-thirds of the total occupant load.

The actual number of exit units that existed at the time of the fire was 16.5* units. (See Table 3.2.) Therefore, exit capacity did not meet the absolute minimum established by the *Life Safety Code*. The maximum permitted occupancy load of the building should have been limited to 1,511 persons, based on the calculations in Table 3.2.

The exact arrangement of the double swinging doors in the Cabaret Room leading from the showroom area to the northeast exit (Exit A) and to the southeast exit (Exit B) could not be determined. A busboy reported that the doors swung in both directions:

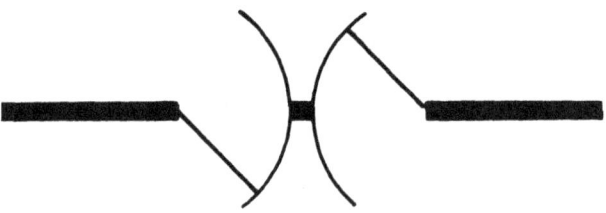

A waitress and another employee were certain that the doors were arranged to swing in one direction only:

Three of the door hinges were found with the remains of the doors at the northeast exitway, and were determined to be double-hinged to allow the doors to swing in both directions. It is possible, however, that

THE BEVERLY HILLS SUPPER CLUB FIRE

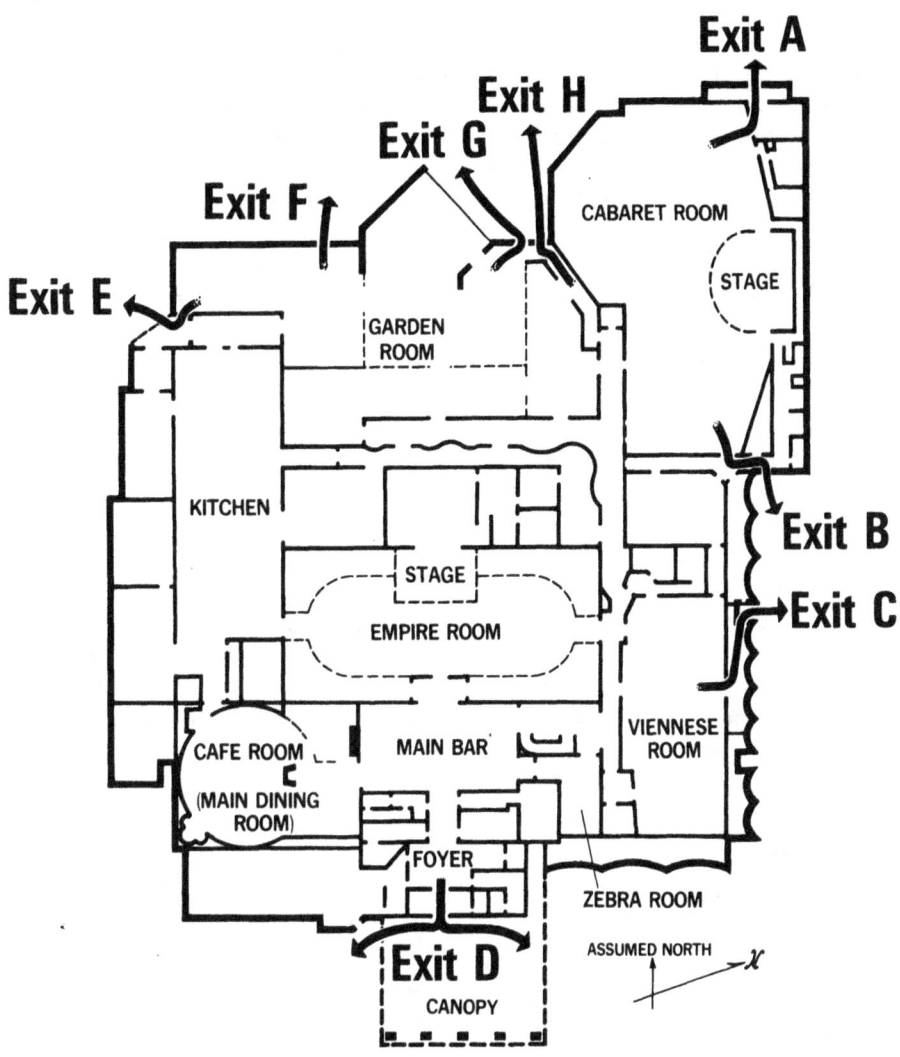

Table 3.2. Beverly Hills Supper Club Building Exits

Exit	Most limiting portion	Exit units Level	Exit units Stairs	Capacity
Exit A	Inside double doors	2 units*	—	200
Exit B	Outside stairs	—	1½ units	112
Exit C	Stairs	—	2½ units	187
Exit D	Inside double doors	2½ units	—	250
Exit E	Stairs	—	1½ units	112
Exit F	Doors	2½ units	—	250
Exit G	Doors	2½ units	—	250
Exit H	Door	1½ units	—	150
	Totals	11 units	5½ units	1,511

Total Building Exit Capacity — 1,511 persons

*Calculations consider that the full width of the inside double doors was usable for egress — see continuing discussion.

the doors were originally installed as double swinging, but at some time were stopped to allow them to swing in one direction only.

The egress analysis was calculated on the basis of double swinging doors at both exits; i.e., occupants had the full use of both doors to escape from the building. If in fact the doors were arranged to swing in one direction only (i.e., only one side of the doors could be used to escape from the building), the means of egress from the building in general and from the Cabaret Room in particular would be even more severely restricted.

The southeast exit (Exit B) was determined to have 1½ units of exit width that would serve 112 persons. The double doors at the southeast corner of the Cabaret Room leading to the exit would have been restricted to one unit of exit width if the doors had been arranged to swing in one direction only as previously described. This restricted access to an exit would not alter the number of exit units at Exit B, as the exit also served other areas in the room such as the backstage area.

The northeast exit (Exit A) would have been reduced from two units of level exit to one unit of level exit, or a capacity of 100. The total building exit capacity would be reduced from 1,511 to 1,411, and the occupant load per room based upon the existing units of exit width would be reduced accordingly.

As previously mentioned, another requirement of the *Life Safety Code* for places of assembly is that every assembly occupancy shall be provided with a main exit of sufficient width to accommodate one-half of the total occupant load. The main exits from the Beverly Hills Supper Club are considered to be the front exit under the canopy "D," and the main north exit from the Garden Rooms "F."

The total units of exit width for the two exits are five units, which would accommodate 500 persons, allowing a total occupant load of 1,000 persons.

Egress From the Second Floor

The *Life Safety Code* requires that every vertical path of exit in a building shall be as suitably enclosed or protected as necessary to afford reasonable safety to occupants while using exits, and to prevent spread of fire, smoke, or fumes through vertical openings from floor to floor before occupants have entered exits (8-3.1). However, the curved stairway located in the Hallway of the Mirrors was neither enclosed nor protected.* Monumental stairs are accepted by the *Life Safety Code* as required exits if all requirements for exit stairs are complied with, including required enclosures. An exception to this is that curved stairs may be accepted with a radius of 25 feet or more at the inner edges. Examination of building plans of the Beverly Hills Supper Club, however, disclosed that the radius of the curved stairs in the Club was less than 25 feet at the inner edges.

Section 5-5.3 of the *Life Safety Code* additionally requires that exit access shall be so arranged that it will not be necessary to travel toward any area of high hazard occupancy in order to reach the nearest exit. However, the west stairway from the second floor to the first floor required occupants to travel through the kitchen to reach the nearest exit. The kitchen is considered an area of high hazard occupancy; therefore, the stairway should have been arranged to discharge to the exterior of the building.

Considering the unenclosed, curved stairway from the east side of the second floor, and the stairway requiring occupants to travel through the kitchen from the west side of the second floor, it is concluded that the second floor had no exits with components permissible by the *Life Safety Code*.

Number of Exits

Investigative information places the estimated population of the Cabaret Room on the evening of the fire between 1,200 and 1,300 people. By definition, the Cabaret Room itself was a Class A place of assembly (1,000 persons or more). The *Life Safety Code* requires that every Class A place of assembly shall have at least four separate exits as remote from each other as practicable. The Cabaret Room should have had a fourth exit to provide the minimum number of exits, in addition to the need for additional exit capacity as shown in Table 3.3.

Exit Access

Section 2-4 of the *Life Safety Code* requires that exits for places of assembly shall be arranged and maintained to provide free and unobstructed egress from all parts of the building or structure at all times when it is occupied. No lock or fastening shall be installed to prevent free escape from the inside of any building.

The *Life Safety Code* requires that means of egress be continuously maintained free of all obstructions or impediments to full instant use in the case of fire or other emergency (17-1.2.1.1).

On-site investigation of the Beverly Hills Supper Club fire and interviews determined that there were chairs and tables stored on the platform outside the

---
*To qualify the curved stairway as an acceptable exit from the second floor, the stairway would have to have been properly enclosed, with the enclosure terminating at the outside of the building.

Table 3.3 Requirements for Units of Exit Width

	Cabaret Room	Garden Rooms	Empire Room	Viennese Rooms	Cafe dining room, bar, foyer, Zebra Room	Crystal Rooms	Totals
Units of exit width directly to outside existing at time of fire	3.5	6.5 1.5[1]	none	2.5	2.5	none	16.5
Distribution of **occupant load** with existing units of exit width[2]	380	455	156	211	217	92	1,511
Minimum **occupant load** based on square feet per occupant	511	636	447	256	623	262	2,735
Additional **units of level exit width** required based on square feet per occupant[3]	2.5	3.0	4.0	1.0	5.5	2.5	18.5[4]
Actual **occupant load** at time of fire (estimated)	1200-1300	305-450[5]	375-425	100-125	200-250	210-250	2,400-2,800
Additional **units of level exit width** required based on actual occupant load[6]	9.0	0	0	0	0	0	9.0
Total additional **units of level exit width** required[7]	11.5	3.0	4.0	1.0	5.5	2.5	27.5[8]

[1]Exit shared by two rooms.
[2]Does not take into consideration par. 8-2.3.2 & 8-2.3.3.
[3]Reflects credit for existing exits plus additional units (assumed level), and includes requirements for 2/3 remote exit and for 50 percent main exit.
[4]Could be reduced by ideal distribution to 14.5.
[5]Includes estimates for kitchen and main hallway.
[6]These are additional required units above those for square footage. (See Note 3.)
[7]Considers both square footage requirement and actual occupancy.
[8]Could be reduced to 23.5 by ideal distribution.

Viennese Rooms that led to steps to double doors in the screen wall (Exit C). Earlier descriptions of exit access discussed evidence of chains and locks on panic hardware and locked doors.

Exit Marking

The *Life Safety Code* states that every exit in a place of assembly shall be clearly visible, or the route to reach the exit shall be conspicuously indicated in such a manner that every occupant will readily know the direction of escape from any point (2-5).

Section 5-10.1.2 of the *Code* requires that exits and access to exits be marked by readily visible signs in all cases where the exit or way to reach it is not immediately visible to the occupants.

The east-west corridor south of the Cabaret Room was not visible from the north-south corridor, according to employee statements. A door to the corridor appeared to be part of the wall paneling, and it was not marked as an exit. Access to Exits A and B was confusing; the way for occupants to reach these exits should have been indicated.

Rapid spread of fire along the main north-south corridor, delay in notifying occupants of the Cabaret

QUESTION 12
Did you notice any of the conditions below in the room you were in?

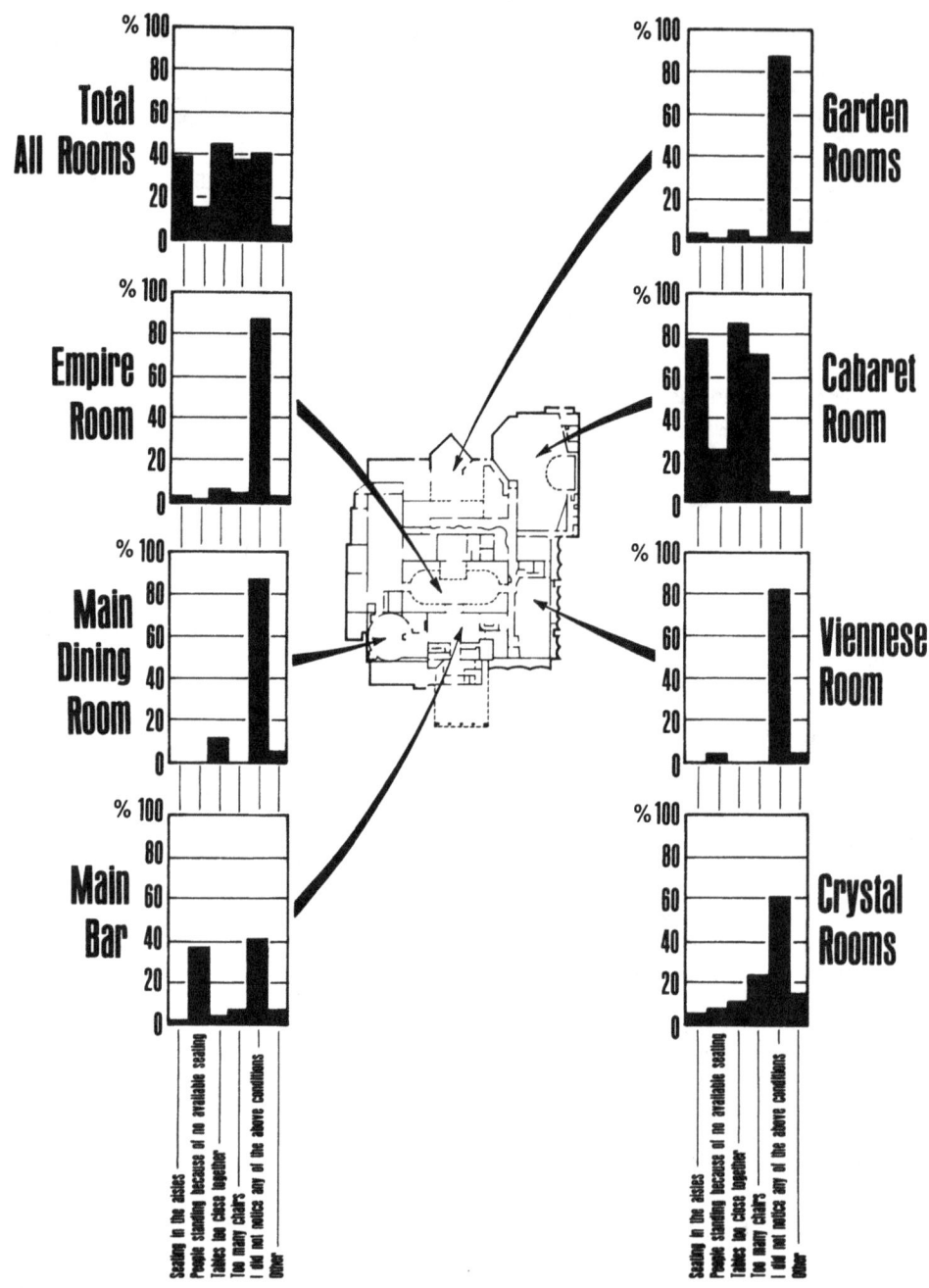

Figure 14.

Room, insufficient exit capacity, and the excessive number of people in the room were all factors that resulted in employees and customers not having enough time to escape.

Part of the means of egress problem in the Cabaret Room that has not been previously discussed was the restricted aisles leading to exits. Section 17-2.6.2 of the *Life Safety Code* requires that the number of seats in places of assembly, where seats are not fastened to the floor, be restricted to not more than one seat for each fifteen square feet of net floor area. The section further requires that adequate aisles to reach exits be maintained at all times.

A large percentage of the occupants in the Cabaret

QUESTION 20
What difficulty was encountered in escaping?

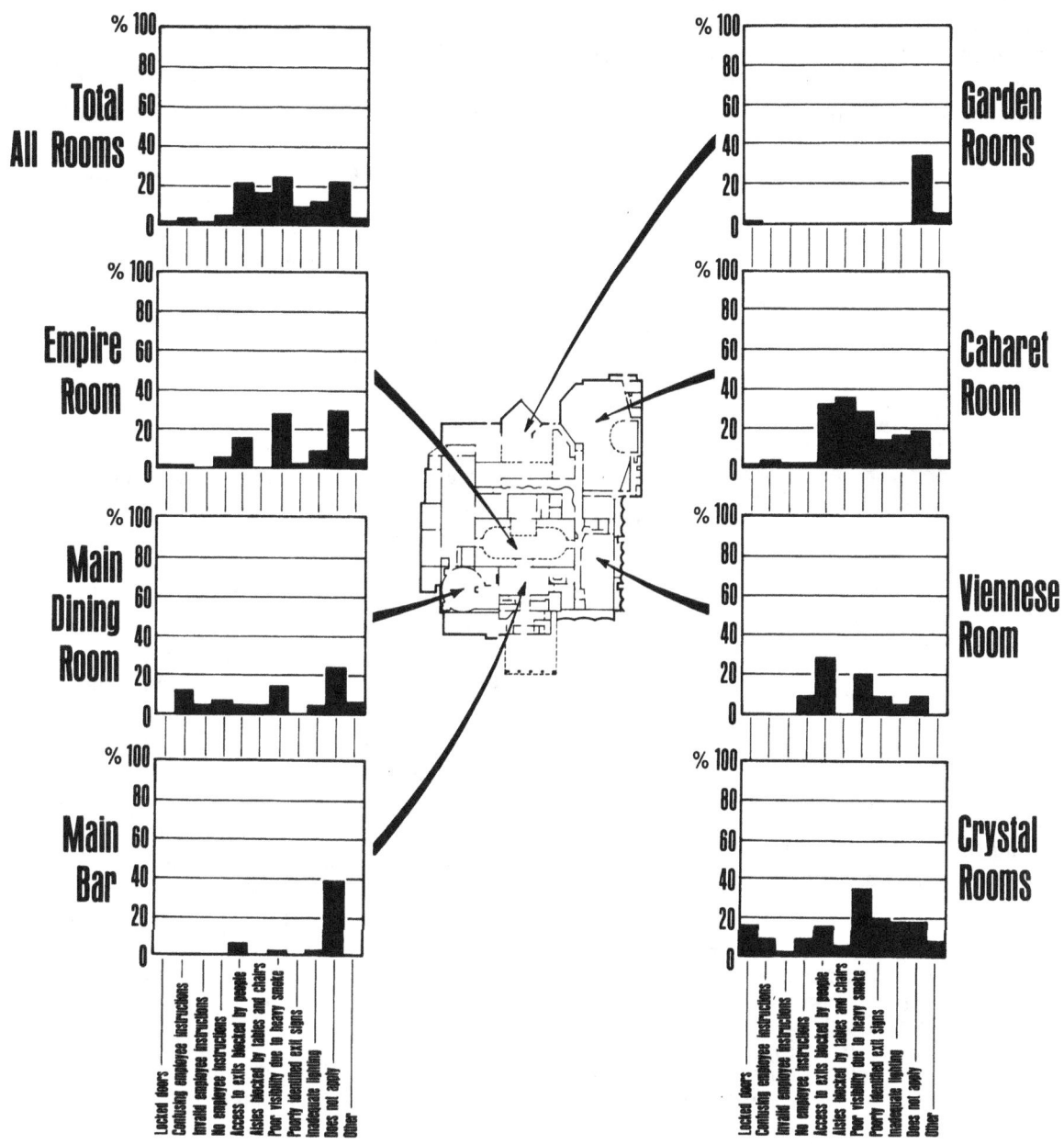

Figure 15.

Room noticed seating in the aisles, tables placed too close together, too many chairs, and other items indicative of restricted aisles. The questionnaire illustrations show the results of the questionnaire data dealing with conditions observed in the various rooms, and indicate that a large percentage of Cabaret Room occupants observed conditions that were not seen in other rooms of the Club. (See Figures 14 and 15.)

Exit Discharge

The features of exit discharge of the Beverly Hills Supper Club, previously discussed in Section I, under "Construction Features of the Club," were: (1) the steep banking to the east of the Club, and (2) the narrow concrete steps beside the loading dock at the kitchen exit (Exit E).

Although reports received soon after the fire stated that people had fallen down the steep banking on the outside of the Club after exiting, these reports could not be substantiated. However, the Newport assistant chief described victims being dragged away from the building when it appeared that the building was about to collapse; this may be the reason that some victims were seen on the side of the slope. Although the exit discharge in the area of Exits B and C was not a documented problem, the steep slope was referred to by a waitress who came out of Exit A.

- .... Once I got outside I couldn't go to my left because there was too many people in front of me, there was a chapel in front of me, and I looked around to the right around the side of the burning building and there were fire trucks already there. Then I thought, 'I guess I'd rather break my neck than to (be) burned to death by these flames,' so I jumped over the cliff and I rolled down the cliff a little ways and I thought I heard somebody calling my name and I pulled myself back up the trees and whatever there was on that hillside, I don't know but I pulled myself back up on the other side of the chapel and I came around to the center of the garden. ...

Other statements referred to exit discharge problems at Exits B and E when people fell from the platform at Exit B and the loading dock at Exit E. A waiter who had exited from the building stated:

- .... I went out the north exit of the kitchen and there is a truck loading dock there and by this time people were coughing pretty much. A couple of people were getting hysterical and they were just falling off the ramp on top of each other. I tried to help a couple of people down, I know I helped the chef down. One lady looked like she was going to pass out, at the top of the steps, and I helped her down.

Other Means of Egress Deviations

There were other deviations from the means of egress requirements of the *Life Safety Code*, but the discrepancies did not have a direct bearing on the fire, and therefore, are not discussed in detail. Briefly, the Cafe dining room and the Crystal Rooms should have had at least two means of egress (8-2.4.3); and because the Cafe dining room and Crystal Rooms had only one means of egress, the arrangement of means of egress was in violation (8-2.5.1). Dead-end travel in excess of 20 feet is not permitted.

Although a detailed analysis was not made, the travel distance from the Empire, Viennese, and Crystal Rooms to an exit was in excess of the 150 feet total length of travel requirement in places of assembly (8-2.6).

The illumination of means of egress was not reported to be a problem, but it is seriously doubted that illumination was provided in the space between the facade and the Viennese Rooms that led to Exit C.

Features of Fire Protection

Although complete sprinkler protection is not required by the *Life Safety Code* in places of assembly located at the level of exit discharge, Section 16-4.2.1.1 of the *Code* requires complete automatic sprinkler protection in windowless areas occupied by 100 or more persons. The Cabaret Room, Empire Room, Viennese Rooms, Cafe dining room, and Crystal Rooms were windowless areas occupied by 100 or more persons, and therefore should have been sprinklered.

Considering the type of construction of the Beverly Hills Supper Club which would limit the capacity of the building to 300 persons;* realizing that the Club was effectively a windowless building;** further considering the windowless area requirement for sprinkler protection; and taking into account that the basic principles for providing proper sprinkler protection include the installation of sprinklers throughout the premises,[14] it is considered that any authority having jurisdiction to enforce the 1976 *Life Safety Code* would have required complete automatic sprinkler protection throughout the Beverly Hills Supper Club.** Additionally, the Beverly Hills Supper Club exceeded the height and area limitations placed on buildings of unprotected, noncombustible construction by the *National Building Code*, and automatic sprinkler protection would be required.

Sprinkler protection in the Beverly Hills Supper Club might or might not have extinguished the fire in

---

*See "Occupant Load."

**With the construction of the false front, or facade, along the portions of the south and east walls of the Beverly Hills Supper Club, the building became, in effect, a windowless building. The Club was not truly windowless, as there were large window areas in the north wall in the area of the Garden Rooms and some small windows in the west wall where the kitchen was located. All showrooms and dining rooms were windowless areas, however, except for the Garden Rooms.

***The Beverly Hills Supper Club exceeded the height and area limitations placed on buildings of unprotected noncombustible construction by the *National Building Code*, and automatic sprinkler protection would be required.

The east wall of the Club, which clearly shows the windowless facade. Exit B is seen in the lower right. (Credit: NFPA)

A view of the south end of the Club. The Canopy is partially visible on the left; the opening in the brick wall is to the Zebra Room. This photo clearly shows how the facade, or false front, was spaced away from the original brick wall, and that the windows in the building were covered. (Credit: NFPA)

A westerly view of the coatroom, or checkroom. Note the wood stud interior partitions and the wood-frame construction of the west wall. The roof over this area was believed to be also of wood construction. (Credit: NFPA)

the Zebra Room, depending on the system installation and the location of the concealed space where the fire originated. A properly installed and maintained sprinkler system would very likely have controlled the fire, however, and certainly would have prevented the spread of fire along the north-south corridor to the Cabaret Room.

Interior Finish

The *Life Safety Code* requires that the interior finish in all means of egress in all places of assembly be Class A (8-3.2.2). Class A interior finish includes any material classified with a flame spread of 0-25. The interior finish in the Hallway of the Mirrors and the main north-south corridor had a flame spread rating greater than 25.

The corridor walls were covered with a decoratively finished, hardboard paneling applied over wood furring strips. This paneling was combustible, and although its flame spread index could not be determined, experience at the National Bureau of Standards[15] indicates that it probably ranged somewhere between 150 and 200.* This paneling was applied to both walls of the corridor for its full length, except for

---

*For representative flame spread indices of similar materials, see *Building Materials Directory,* Underwriters Laboratories Inc. [16]

the curvilinear wall at the west cross corridor, which was of exposed brick, and another section of the corridor near the Cabaret Room, which was paneled on one side with interior doors placed side by side.

Building Service Equipment

It was determined that the most probable cause of ignition was electrical in nature, as discussed in other sections of this report. The electrical service in the Beverly Hills Supper Club that was not destroyed by the fire was therefore thoroughly examined during the investigation. A discussion of the results of this investigation is warranted.

A great deal of time was spent investigating electrical fixtures, wiring, and electrical service at the Club to determine a possible link with the suspected origin of the fire. Due to severe or total destruction of much of the electrical wiring on the first and second floor, a detailed inspection could not be made. Electrical wiring for lights and power in the basement area was 80 percent intact, and damage to this area appears to have been from secondary fires and from heat transmitted through electrical conduit.

The dates when the original electrical wiring installation was completed are unknown, but wiring methods employed date to the period between 1940 and 1970. The original installation appears to have been adequate for the area and electrical load at that time. As additional demands for light and power were made, this load was added to with little or no electrical engineering employed for correct installation, supply, and load factors as set forth in the *National Electrical Code*.[17] Wiring methods employed were also found to be in violation of the *National Electrical Code* requirements. These violations included: transformer and vault room construction, subpanels, wire size, overcurrent protection, emergency power system, open junction boxes, concealed junction boxes, and securing and supporting outlet boxes, cable, and conduit.

Information as to load distributions was unknown, as subpanels were not marked or were improperly marked, and maintenance personnel or electricians with knowledge of the system were not available.

Operating Features

Patrons and employees in the Cabaret Room did not have adequate time to exit from the building. Notification to the Cabaret Room occupants was delayed due to: (1) the lack of a fire alarm system in the building, (2) the lack of an emergency evacuation plan, and (3) the lack of employee training.

In retrospect, a fire alarm system in the Beverly Hills Supper Club could have been effective in providing an early warning to all occupants, and could have avoided the disastrous delay of alerting staff and occupants of the Cabaret Room. The *Life Safety Code* does not require an alarm system in places of assembly.*

The *Life Safety Code* does require that employees be trained and drilled in the duties they are to perform in case of fire, panic, or other emergency in order to be of greatest service in effecting orderly exit of occupants. An evacuation plan of the Beverly Hills Supper Club that assigned specific responsibilities to employees, covered all areas of the building, and stressed the need to evacuate customers immediately on the alarm of a fire, would possibly have provided the additional minutes that would have been necessary to evacuate all occupants from the building. It was determined during the investigation of the Beverly Hills Supper Club fire that employees were not schooled or drilled in duties to be performed during a fire or panic situation.

*Many authorities believe that the use of alarm sounding devices (gongs, sirens, etc.), in places of public assembly in buildings in which fire exit drills are not feasible may create panic conditions, and recommend visual signals, coded lights, or other devices for alerting personnel responsible for an orderly evacuation of the building in the event of an emergency. Although the *Life Safety Code* does not require an alarm system in places of assembly, the best means of alerting occupants to a fire emergency without creating hysterical or other ineffective escape behavior should be investigated. See "Recommended Areas for Further Study."

Another less obvious reason why there was not adequate warning to the Cabaret Room occupants is the physical size of the Club, the arrangement of the rooms in the Club, and the movement of employees within the complex.

• OBSERVATION: A definite pattern was observed in the employee actions described in the transcripts — that employees, when made aware of the fire emergency, returned to the room and party that they had been serving prior to the notification. Employees made certain that their rooms or their parties exited to safety, and seemed to assume a responsibility for those customers they were serving, but not necessarily for customers in other parts of the building.

Although there was no emergency plan at the Beverly Hills Supper Club to notify patrons and no alarm system, the word of the fire emergency was spread rapidly throughout the Club with the exception of the Cabaret Room. The Cafe dining room and the main bar were close enough to the area of origin of the fire for the occupants to see smoke and hear the first reports of the fire in time to evacuate in relative safety. The Crystal Rooms on the second floor, where two occupants died, also received early notice, but those rooms were located directly above the open stairway outside the Zebra Room, and alternate means of escape were severely restricted. Occupants of other areas of the building — the Empire Room, Viennese Rooms, Garden Rooms, and kitchen — were notified by employees who were in the area of the Zebra Room or were in the kitchen or service halls, and saw and overheard other employees running for extinguishers or notifying the manager.

The exception to this word-of-mouth notification was the Cabaret Room, which was isolated from the rest of the Club once the show was in progress. In other words, there were no waiters, waitresses, busboys, or hostesses from the Cabaret Room traveling to and from the kitchen or standing in the service halls taking a break between dining room seatings.

Descriptions of employee actions in the transcripts indicated that employees attempting to notify the managers of the Club traveled through the main north-south corridor and the service halls, and into the kitchen, while other persons traveled through the kitchen, main dining area, and main bar. In that process, and in the search for extinguishers, the adjacent rooms were alerted and evacuation of the building was begun.

Such was apparently not the case in the Cabaret Room. No employees were in a position to see or hear the activity in the corridors, and they were not aware of the hazardous situation. They therefore did not alert the patrons to evacuate until the busboy entered

QUESTION 8
Approximately what time was it when you first observed smoke?

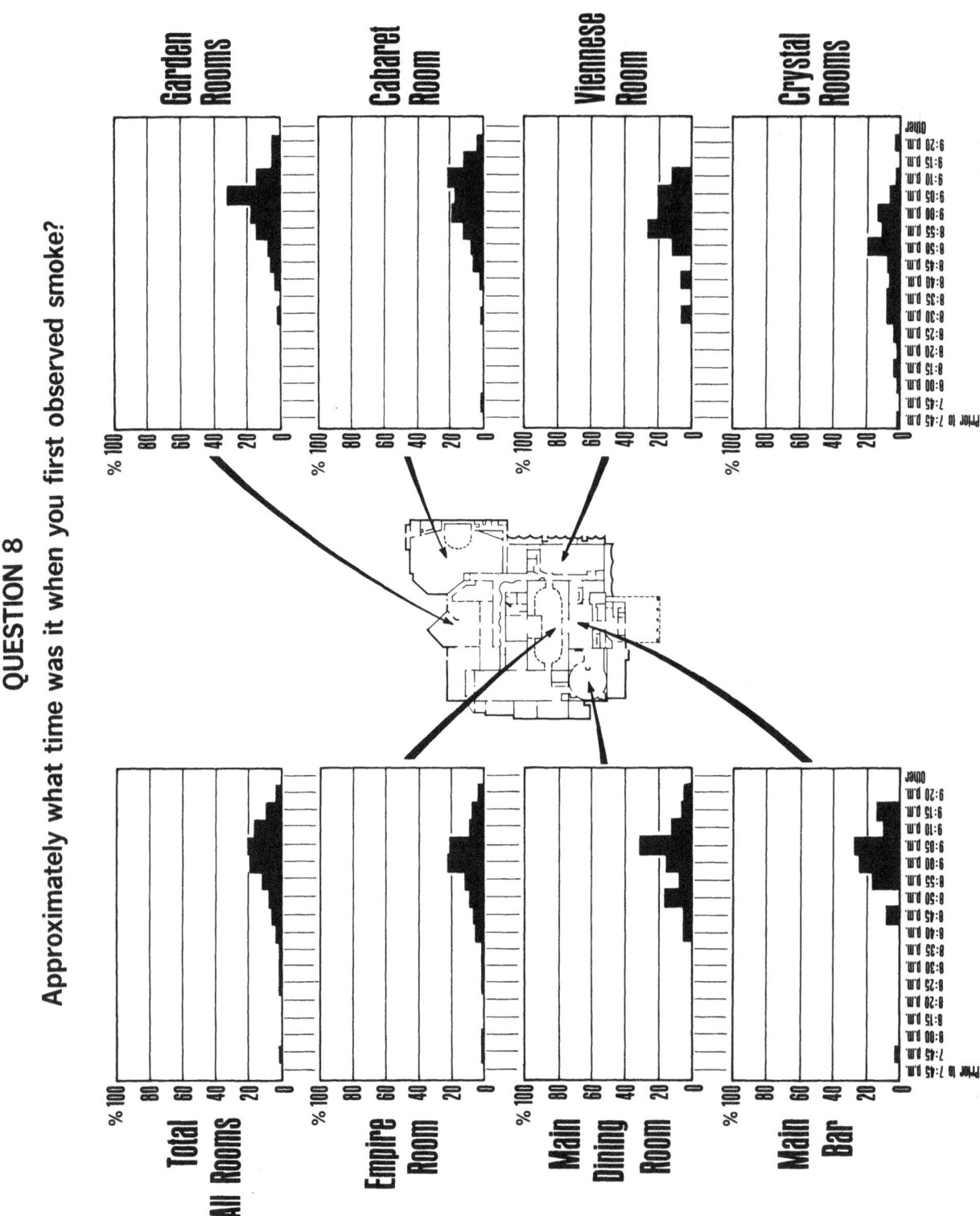

Figure 16.

the Cabaret Room and made the announcement from the stage. It is interesting to note that the busboy worked in various rooms of the Club and had no permanently assigned station. Also, it should be noted that he worked in the Cabaret Room prior to going to the Viennese Rooms to help with a party there.

The size of the Club obviously tended to increase the isolation of the Cabaret Room from the rest of the building because the Cabaret Room was equipped with its own dishwashing facility and bars. These facilities were most likely provided because of the distance between the Cabaret Room and other areas, including the kitchen and other bars.

HUMAN BEHAVIOR

In the analysis of human behavior exhibited at the Beverly Hills Supper Club fire, it was more practicable to explore human actions during the fire than it was to examine human motivation. The human actions could be broken down into two "events," or actions relating to human behavior, which began with perception of the fire and led to the actions taken by individuals, based upon their perceptions of the fire. In the analysis of human behavior, the survey and the interview statements were used as the data source. The data source consisted of 1,117 completed questionnaires and 630 interviews that were conducted, taped, and transcribed by the Kentucky State Police. The NFPA then selected a random sample of 20 percent of the available interviews of building occupants (employees, patrons, and others) who were present in each of the rooms the night of the Beverly Hills Supper Club fire. To this data were added eighteen interviews of key personnel from the management and staff of the club, and from fire officers who responded to the emergency. Statistical validity cannot be ascribed to frequencies, correlations, and ratios obtained, but questions can be asked, inferences can be drawn (as long as these inferences do not have confidence levels ascribed to them), and hypotheses can be deduced. From this effort, these hypotheses can then be tested with new data* to test what actions or variations in actions may make a difference in future fires in similar occupancies.

Questionnaire Data

It is interesting to examine the distribution of times that occcupants (patrons or employees) first saw fire or smoke. (See Table 3.4.) The range of times for "first observed smoke" was from before 7:45 p.m.

*New data may be drawn from many sources, including past large fires, observed fire drills, tests, and simulations.

Table 3.4 Comparison of Question 8 And Question 10 Replies

| Room | When did you first observe | | | |
| | Smoke? | | Fire? | |
	Median	Range	Median	Range
Crystal	8:50	7:45-9:20	9:00	8:30-9:20
Viennese	8:55	8:30-9:10	9:10	8:30-9:20
Cabaret	9:00	7:45-9:20	9:10	8:30-9:20
Empire	9:00	7:45-9:20	9:10	8:30-9:20
Main bar	9:02	7:45-9:15	9:20	8:30-9:20
Main dining	9:05	8:40-9:20	9:15	8:50-9:20
Garden	9:05	8:30-9:20	9:05	8:35-9:20
All rooms	9:00	7:45-9:20	9:10	8:30-9:20

(one person) to 9:20 p.m. (twenty-eight persons). The range of times for "first observed fire" was from 8:30 p.m. (fourteen persons) to 9:20 p.m. (188 persons). These are the ranges of times indicated on the questionnaires. All respondents reported that they saw smoke, although 203 reported that they "did not observe fire." While there were many variations in time of perception within and among rooms, the median time that occupants "first observed smoke" (see Figure 16) was 9:00 p.m.; for those who did observe fire, the median time of "first observed fire" was 9:10 p.m., which is consistent with the reconstruction of the fire by the fire investigation team. *No respondents* stated that they *first* became aware of the fire (from all sources, including fire and smoke) by answering "I saw fire"; only 6 percent became aware from "seeing or smelling smoke"; and 78 percent answered that they became aware by "an employee mentioned it." Sixty-two percent believed that when they first became aware of the fire, the fire was slightly, moderately, or extremely serious; 60 percent of the respondents answered that they observed one or more of the following hazardous conditions:

- Seating in the aisles.
- People standing because of no available seating.
- Too many chairs.
- Other (8 percent saw other items they specified as hazardous).

Most people were aware of an emergency, as 87 percent of 1,050 people responding saw fire or smoke within five minutes of being alerted. (See Table A.6.) However, the seriousness of the situation seems not to have been perceived by anyone until the ensuing gray-black smoke was observed. (See also next section, titled "Interviews.")

In another vein, it is interesting that 88 percent of the 1,092 persons responding to Question 19 had *no* difficulty locating an exit. (See Figure 17 and Table A.9.) This is quite important if one considers that of

QUESTION 19
Did you have difficulty in locating an exit?

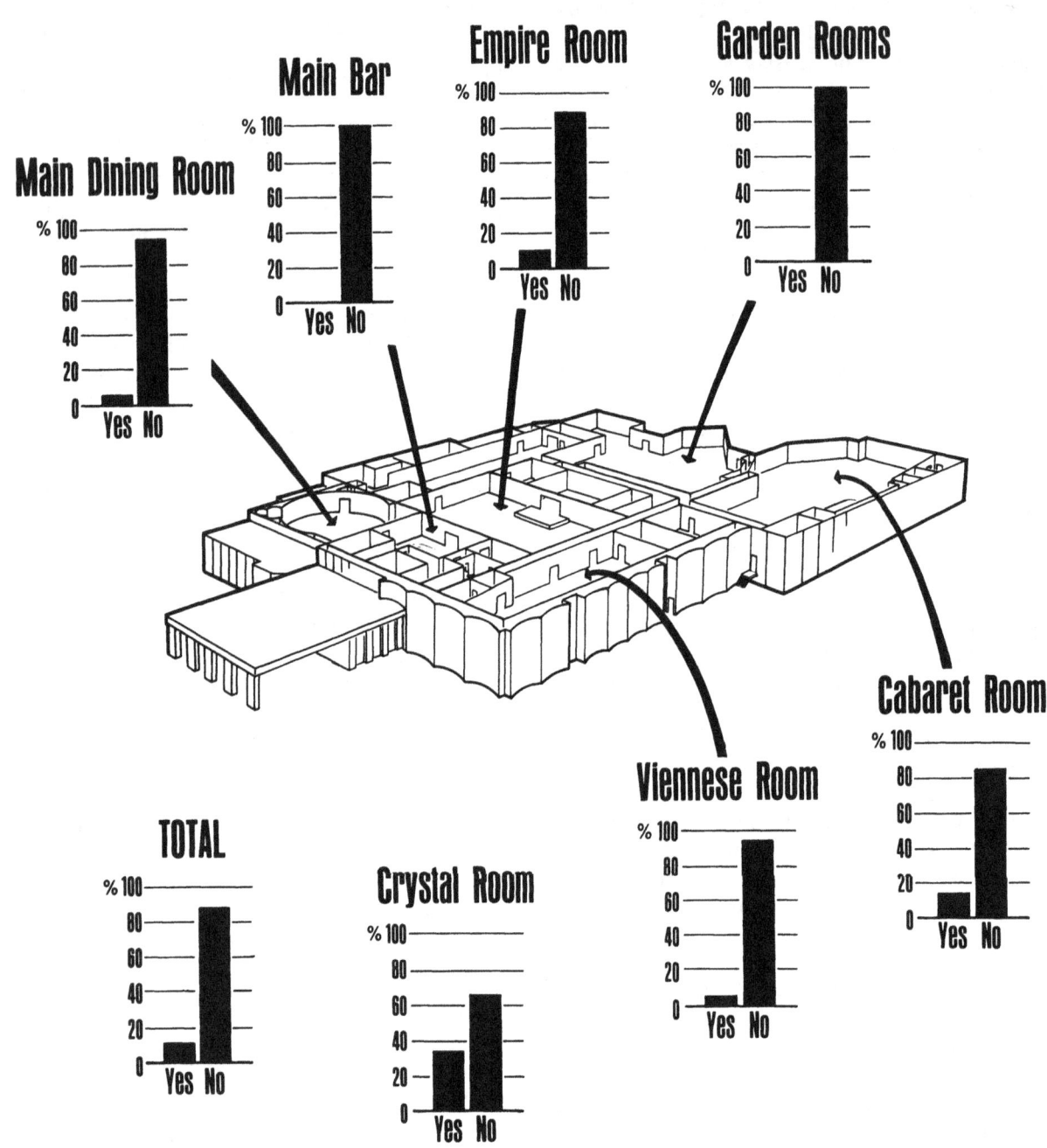

Figure 17.

the 1,117 respondents, 76 percent reported that an employee assisted them in exiting from their room and/or the building. Does this imply that employees were generally concerned for, and directly assisted, patrons? This seemed to be the case in that of the 78 percent (871) who indicated difficulty in escaping (of the 1,117 respondents), only 8 percent (seventy) reported that any of these difficulties in escaping were related to employee actions; i.e., confusing employee instructions, invalid employee instructions, or no employee instructions. The conclusion that employees did indeed assist in the orderly escape will be further supported by statements made in the analysis of interview transcripts.

In general, it seems clear from the respondents that most patrons and staff were probably not truly aware of the seriousness of the emergency and exited, for the most part, with little difficulty. Where exiting difficulties occurred, they related principally to the crowded conditions aggravated by the heavy smoke. Where needed, individuals generally obtained assistance from staff personnel (employees). The inferences that arise are that employees such as waiters, waitresses, and maîtres d'hôtel react in an "other"* interest fashion in an emergency such as this one.

Interviews

Interviews were carefully reviewed to determine what the people who were in the Club or who responded to the emergency perceived to be true and what actions they took. From a careful reading, a pervasive theme is that generally patron and staff alike did not believe the emergency was serious. This is in contrast to what they reported on questionnaires. There is, in fact, no statement by anyone that they believed the emergency serious until they were directly confronted with thick, black, eye-irritating smoke. Even then, they moved in a quiet fashion toward exits until the last moment when a rush of hot, searing gases and flames rolled through the Cabaret Room. Even then, what has often been termed "panic" seems not to have occurred.** A few quotations should help in clarifying what is meant:

Person One

- There was flame and smoke and it just rolled into the room and it was the blackest smoke I'd seen ever. The only way, if you could just take oil and just get it to roll in mid-air then that was the way the smoke was. I knew at that time, I was going to die and up until that time, everybody was orderly. There wasn't any chaos, no screaming, no panicking or anything. It was when the people saw the smoke and the fire that they became panicky and they started screaming. I knew that this was it, that we were going to die.

    So it wasn't a question of people trying to figure out why did a hundred and sixty-one (sic) people die. They died because there wasn't enough time to get them out. That's why they died. If there had of been three more minutes, those people could have gotten out. Not as many people could have gotten out that did get out had they been in panic. That's why I will continue to say there was no panic. The people were orderly. They got out in an orderly fashion up until the smoke and fire came and you wouldn't have been human if you didn't scream then because they were dying.

Person Two

- We weren't a minute too soon. . . . The people after us were just falling out of the door. I mean literally falling all over the ground.

    No, I think this must have happened when the panic started and the panic started when the flames shot through. People just started rushing for the exits. We kind of got in at the beginning of the panic, so I didn't see any of this.

Person Three

- There was very little shoving. The shoving was of a constructive shove. It was shoving to move people faster, you know, you can move faster if someone's pushing you a little bit, helping you out, there was no like destructive type of thing where you were just taking people away and going in front of them or anything like that. It was orderly.

If there was no panic until seconds before fire and smoke felled people, and there are no statements of so-called panic from any but those who witnessed the death-delivering wave of hot gases into the Cabaret Room, what might be concluded? First of all, it seems reasonable when reading all of the statements that it might be well to discard the term "panic" for a more descriptive term with less emotional, connotative values. That is, if people were pushing others out of

---

*"Other"-serving actions are defined as actions principally intended to assist others in removing themselves from danger.

**Schultz has defined panic as "a fear-induced flight behavior which is non-rational, non-adaptive, and non-social, which serves to reduce the escape possibilities of the group as a whole."[18] In discussing Schultz's definition, Wood notes, "He (Schultz) starts by offering a definition of the term 'panic' making the point that the word has been and is, often misused in describing the behavior of people fleeing from danger. In many cases, this flight is the only rational way in which to respond, the critical difference between rational escape behavior and non-rational, panic, behaviour being in the manner in which we try to effect escape."[19]

the way or knocking them down and walking on them, then it should be described that way. If people were screaming, then one should state whether they were screaming for help, for loved ones, or just screaming uncontrollably and were therefore not able to help themselves or others escape from the emergency. While the term "panic" is used many ways, it is most often used as a reason for certain actions; in particular, as the reason for giving a warning to patrons or as a reason for delivering directions in a manner to assure calm and orderly exit from a structure. Secondly, it seems reasonable to conclude that some mechanisms were at work that minimized the potential for hysterical, noncooperative actions, and encouraged the very cooperative, altruistic behavior actually observed. One of these seems to be a *lack of appreciation for the seriousness of the emergency.*

A second reason seems to be the role acceptance of all involved. Constantly, employees worked through directions and encouragement to safely evacuate those persons they served, i.e., waitresses their station, function supervisors and bartenders their rooms, busboys the rooms they served, and at least for one top manager, the building. There were almost no exceptions to this rule. In line with this, patrons consistently took the instructions of staff personnel with minor exceptions; for example, where it was clear to one patron that his party could not exit the Cabaret Room safely since they were last in the queues to use the emergency exits, he took the calculated risk to exit his party through the smoke in the main north-south corridor and to the Garden Rooms exit. An interesting study in role acceptance[20] was exemplified by an experienced professional fire fighter who assumed the role of patron until he and his party were outside; once outside, he assumed the role of fire fighter and began rescue operations.

To test this observation that the role of the person at the time of the fire determined the individual's behavior, a quantitative study was made of 119 interviews of people who were in the building when the fire began. These interviews were split among three analysts. The analysts were instructed to count all actions by occupants from the time they became aware of the emergency to the time they exited, and to count the number of times the action fell into one of the following categories:

1. *"Self"-serving actions.* Actions designed principally to remove the individual from danger.
2. *"Other"-serving actions.* Actions designed principally to assist others in removing themselves from danger.
3. *"Other" actions.* Actions that were intended to get information about or reduce criticality of the

Table 3.5 Chi-Square Test of Occupant Actions*

	Actions more "self"-serving		Actions more "other"-serving		Total
	Number	Percent of total	Number	Percent of total	
Patron	25	92.6%	2	7.4%	27
Employee	3	15.8%	16	84.2%	19
	28		18		46

*x^2 = 27.65: significant at .001

emergency, but not to directly assist others, e.g., see what the problem was or call the fire department.

These were then scored by simply computing whether the number of "self"-serving actions were less than, equal to, or greater than the "other"-serving actions. A Chi-Square test[21] was run on a sample of forty-six occupants (see Table 3.5) to test the hypothesis that employees are "other"-serving and patrons are "self"-serving. On the basis of this test, one could say that the hypothesis is true with a confidence that this conclusion would not be wrong more than one time in a thousand. Role acceptance at the Beverly Hills Supper Club was real, and precisely what one might expect it would be.

Why was this role acceptance apparently effective in maintaining an orderly egress from the building? From the interview data, it seems clear that the employees continually provided information on what to do and how to do it. By this, it is meant that the employees consistently presented directions such as "This way out," or "Stay calm and we'll all get out," and patrons apparently accepted the instructions of the employees as if they were group leaders.[22]

Exit Analysis

In order to test the opinions voiced by interviewees — that there just was not enough time to get out of the exits — a computer study was conducted. Inputs to this study were:

• All doors and openings into or within the structure provided potential escape routes. This was termed "design potential."

• All doors not locked at the time of the fire and openings into or within the structure. This was termed "prefire."

• Layout of the structure and design features significant to fire development and/or flame spread.

• The best scenario when the safe passage by persons not wearing self-contained breathing apparatus was blocked by smoke or other products of combustion.

Table 3.6 Degradation of Escape Routes From Listed Location

			Number of directed escape routes				
	Location	Design potential	Prefire	8:45-8:50	8:55-9:00	9:00-9:05	9:10
1	Crystal Rooms	62	36	16	0	0	0
2	Crystal Rooms	41	29	16	0	0	0
3	Main staircase	72	45	0	0	0	0
4	Upstairs hallway	41	29	16	0	0	0
5	Cabaret Room	43	31	11	5	0	0
6	Garden Rooms	19	17	7	3	0	0
7	Corridor	54	48	0	0	0	0
8	Corridor	39	22	17	0	0	0
9	Corridor	43	31	11	5	0	0
10	Viennese Rooms	61	43	17	0	0	0
11	Empire Room	31	21	18	10	2	0
12	Main bar	58	39	0	0	0	0
13	Zebra Room	118	82	0	0	0	0
14	Main dining room	47	35	16	0	0	0
15	Kitchen	40	32	16	5	1	0
16	Dishwashing	23	19	11	6	2	0

The results of the simulation are shown in Table 3.6. (See also Figure 18.) The output shows the following:

• *Zebra:* Prior to the fire, if all doors are unlocked, 118 paths from the Zebra Room always moving away from the room of origin and toward some exit to the outside.

— Prior to the fire, with the doors that were locked at that time, 82 paths.
— Sometime between 8:45 p.m. and 8:50 p.m., no paths.

• *Crystal (1):* There are rooms with permanent walls on either side of the hall.

— Prior to the fire, design potential, 62 paths.
— Prior to the fire, prefire, 36 paths.
— 8:45 p.m. to 8:50 p.m., 16 paths.
— 8:55 p.m. to 9:00 p.m., no paths.

• *Crystal (2):*

— Prior to the fire, design potential, 41 paths.
— Prior to the fire, prefire, 29 paths.
— 8:45 p.m. to 8:50 p.m., 16 paths.
— 8:55 p.m. to 9:00 p.m., no paths.

• *Cabaret*

— Prior to the fire, design potential, 43 paths.
— 8:45 p.m. to 8:50 p.m., 11 paths.
— 8:55 p.m. to 9:00 p.m., 5 paths.
— 9:00 p.m. to 9:05 p.m., no paths.

The conclusions are rather straightforward.

• *Zebra:* The rather trivial result (since it was an input) that just after the party left, the room was untenable.

• *Crystal 1 and 2:* Sometime between 8:55 p.m. and 9:00 p.m., the number of escape-route options was reduced from sixteen to zero.

• *Cabaret:* Sometime between 9:00 p.m. and 9:05 p.m., the escape options narrowed from five to zero.

This squares quite well with the testimony and with others that the occupants of these rooms had about five minutes to exit these rooms. Note, however, that persons who had left the Cabaret or Crystal Rooms and were in the kitchen or Garden Rooms had approximately another five minutes to escape. While the Cabaret Room was perceived to be a long way from the fire, in terms of time it was very close to the emergency. In terms of human behavior, this indicates that persons, particularly those responsible for patron safety, must learn to view the relationship of one area to another in terms of unimpeded access (i.e., no barriers) — not in terms of distance — so that alerting and evacuation priority decisions can be made effectively. That owners and employees perceived the Cabaret Room as a long way away in terms of time as well as distance is not surprising and is, in fact, consistently supported by numerous comments in testimony in two ways: (1) the complete surprise that fire and/or smoke could travel and/or develop so rapidly, and (2) comments concerning the service problems due to distance for this area; for example, the setting up of service bars in the area, the difficulty in carrying food back to this area, and the time consumed in walking back to this area for various reasons.

CONCLUSIONS AND FINDINGS

Major Contributing Factors to the Large Loss of Life

The population of the Beverly Hills Supper Club at the time of the fire was approximately 2,400 to 2,800, and about 1,200 to 1,300 of those persons were in the Cabaret Room. Occupants in the Cabaret Room were not notified of the fire until most of the other occupants in the building had evacuated to safety. When the Cabaret Room occupants were made aware of the fire emergency, they did not have adequate time nor sufficient egress capacity provided for occupants to escape from the building. They were overcome by fire gases and smoke. Of the 164 fatalities, nearly all were occupants of the Cabaret Room. The following conclusions are considered the major contributing factors to the large loss of life:

- The fire in the Zebra Room developed for a considerable time, and discovery was delayed. The presence of concealed, combustible ceiling tile and wood materials used for supports provided a fuel supply for continued spread of the fire through the original and other concealed spaces. Following discovery, this fire posed a severe threat to occupants.

- The Beverly Hills Supper Club staff attempted to extinguish the fire before notifying occupants to evacuate from the building and prior to calling the fire department. There was no evacuation plan establishing fire emergency procedures for the Beverly Hills Supper Club, and employees were not schooled or drilled in duties they were to perform in case of fire.

- The number of people in the Cabaret Room exceeded by about triple* the number of occupants that the room could safely accommodate. Also, the number of occupants in the Beverly Hills Supper Club (total building) on the night of the fire exceeded by about double* the number of people that the building could safely accommodate.

- The capacity of the means of egress for the Club and especially for the Cabaret Room was not adequate for the occupant load based on square feet per occupant, or for the actual number of occupants that were in the building at the time of the fire.

- The interior finish in the main north-south corridor exceeded the flame spread allowed for places of assembly in the *Life Safety Code*, and contributed to the rapid spread of fire from the Zebra Room to the Cabaret Room.

- The Beverly Hills Supper Club was not provided with automatic sprinkler protection as required by codes in effect at the time of the fire:

— With the construction of the false wall or facade along parts of the south and east sides of the building, the Beverly Hills Supper Club became effectively a windowless building, and many rooms in the Club were windowless areas. The *Life Safety Code* requires automatic sprinkler protection for such areas.

— The Beverly Hills Supper Club exceeded the height and area limitations placed on buildings of unprotected noncombustible construction by the *National Building Code,* and automatic sprinkler protection would be required.

Other Significant Findings of the Investigation

Other significant findings of the investigation, in addition to the major conclusions listed in the previous section, are listed as follows:

- There was no fire alarm system in the Beverly Hills Supper Club. Although not required by the *Life Safety Code,* a fire alarm system could have been effective in providing a warning to all occupants; the best means of alerting occupants of places of assembly to produce effective and orderly evacuation performance should be investigated. (See "Recommended Areas for Further Study.")

- The Beverly Hills Supper Club had numerous and serious deviations from the means of egress requirements of the *Life Safety Code*. Deviations included exit access, exits, exit marking, and exit discharge.

- The *Life Safety Code* in effect in Kentucky at the time of the fire could have avoided this large loss of life if it had been applied to eliminate significant deviations contributing to the loss of life.

- The Beverly Hills Supper Club was essentially of unprotected, noncombustible construction. This construction type is not permitted for Class A places of assembly (1,000 or more persons) by the *Life Safety Code.*

- Evacuation of the Beverly Hills Supper Club was calm and orderly without the disorderly behavior often termed "panic" until thick, black smoke entered the areas where occupants were exiting. Panic is not considered a major contributing factor to the large loss of life, but such behavior probably did occur when people knew they could not escape.

- Employees and patrons observed and encountered smoke as they left the building, but did not see fire inside the Club (except for a very few who saw fire in the Zebra Room, and occupants of the Cabaret Room who saw flames enter the room.)

---

*The number of people the building and room could safely accommodate is based on distribution of occupant load with existing units of exit width. See Table 3.3.

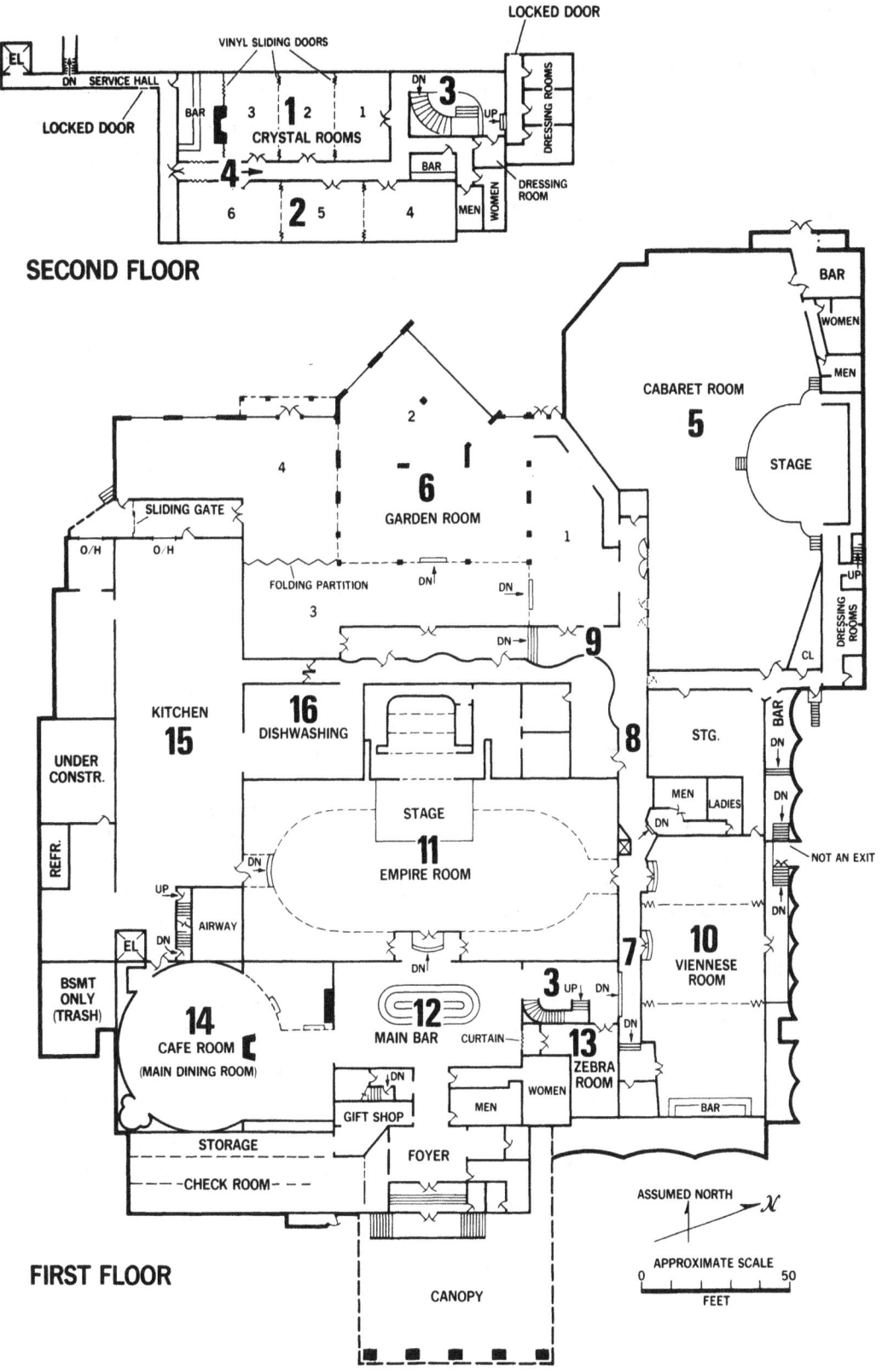

FIGURE IV-D-4 - ROOM DEFINITIONS FOR EXIT ANALYSIS

Figure 18.

- Employees of the Club were not trained or drilled in emergency procedures, but did respond to the fire emergency remarkably well. They notified patrons of the fire, directed them to exits, and generally assisted people to escape from the building.

- Fire fighters did not have early notification of the fire and did not have time to locate and confine the fire before smoke and fire had entered the Cabaret Room, resulting in the large loss of life.

- Heroic rescue actions of employees and fire fighters saved many lives of persons trapped in the Cabaret Room who would otherwise have perished.

RECOMMENDED AREAS FOR FURTHER STUDY

Earlier the question was posed as to why the patrons did not evacuate sooner if they detected smoke or fire as early as they said and considered the emergency to be fairly severe when they first became aware of the fire. A possible answer was given; namely, that the comments given to trained interrogators belie this concern. Indeed, the vast majority of people who exited successfully greatly underestimated the risk. Another possible answer is given; namely, the staff personnel of the Beverly Hills Supper Club assumed the responsibility (leadership role) for guiding and assisting those they served in an exemplary manner. The third possible explanation involves a remarkable lack of what is termed "panic." Why, then, if patron and employee alike performed in what would seem to be a very effective manner, did 164 persons die? From a behavioral viewpoint, this question must be addressed under the assumption that the fire did occur and no changes are to be made in the physical environment. From this perspective, a possible immediate notification to evacuate all rooms may well have saved all persons, including the two who died in the dressing room off the Crystal Rooms.

It should not be inferred from the preceding that there are no nagging behavioral questions to be asked. Indeed there are, and principal among them are:

- **The role of risk perception in effective escape behavior.**

Given: The assessment of risk by almost all involved, up until the final moments in the structure, was well below the actual risk.

Question: What other factors; e.g., ambiguity of visual and olfactory clues, or past successful experience in putting out fires with hand extinguishers, must be overcome in assessing and reporting fire emergencies, and how should this be done?

Question: If patrons and employees had accurately assessed the risk, would hysterical and less than altruistic behavior have appeared and led to more casualties?

Question: How does one present the actual risk to occupants, staff, or patron to ensure immediate action, but at the same time minimize the occurrence of hysterical or other ineffective escape behavior?

Question: What is the importance of continual positive reinforcement by persons in authority, in this case the Club employees, in maintaining calm but determined escape behavior?

Question: What are the alternatives to, and the effectiveness of, other means to provide constant escape information to persons attempting to leave a fire emergency?

- **Role acceptance and fire emergency behavior.**

Given: The roles of patron or employee were determining factors in effective escape action in this particular fire.

Question: Would similar effective behavior be experienced in other supper clubs?

Question: Would similar effective behavior be demonstrated through role acceptance by staff and public in other public assembly occupancies?[23]

Question: How does role acceptance relate to effective fire behavior in general?

Question: How does one utilize the concept of role in developing firesafety plans? Designing firesafe structures?

Question: What are the implications of role in the form, content, and purpose of firesafety educational materials and programs?

- **Related questions.**

Given: The behavior was as described earlier.

Question: How much of the difference in patron versus employee behavior should be ascribed to the use of alcohol by patrons?

Question: How much of the difference in patron versus employee fatalities and other injuries were due to familiarity with the structure?

Question: How strongly does occupation, sex, and personal reasons (loved one or personal belongings left behind) affect re-entry behavior?

Question: How much of the role assumption differences, e.g., fire fighting, guiding, rescuing, and assisting, should be ascribed to male versus female role perceptions?

NOTES

[1] *Investigative Report To The Governor — Beverly Hills Supper Club Fire, May 28, 1977,* Commonwealth of Kentucky, Frankfort, Kentucky, September 16, 1977.

[2] Bright, Richard G., *Beverly Hills Supper Club Fire, Southgate, Kentucky, May 28, 1977 — An Analysis of the Development and Spread of Fire from the Room of Fire Origin (Zebra Room) to the Cabaret Room,* U.S. Department of Commerce, National Bureau of Standards, Washington, DC, September 1, 1977. (See Appendix C.)*

[3] "Legal Analysis — General Considerations," *Investigative Report To The Governor — Beverly Hills Supper Club Fire,* Commonwealth of Kentucky, Frankfort, Kentucky, September 16, 1977.

[4] Bright, Richard G., *Analysis of the Development and Spread of Fire.*

[5] *Officer's Handbook for Determining Cause and Circumstances of Fire,* NFPA FIFI-4, National Fire Protection Association, Boston, 1974.

[6] Bright, Richard G., *Analysis of the Development and Spread of Fire.*

[7] *Ibid.*

[8] *Ibid.*

[9] *Ibid.*

[10] *Ibid.*

[11] *Ibid.*

[12] *Ibid.*

[13] NFPA 101, *Code for Safety to Life from Fire in Buildings and Structures,* National Fire Protection Association, Boston, 1976.

[14] NFPA 13, *Standard for the Installation of Sprinkler Systems,* National Fire Protection Association, Boston, 1976.

[15] Bright, Richard G., *Analysis of the Development and Spread of Fire.*

[16] *Building Materials Directory,* Underwriters Laboratories Inc., Chicago, January 1976, p. 174.

[17] NFPA 70, *National Electrical Code,* National Fire Protection Association, Boston, 1975.

[18] Schultz, D. P., *An Experimental Approach to Panic Behavior,* Office of Naval Research, Department of the Navy, Arlington, VA, 1966.

[19] Wood, P. G., "The Behavior of People in Fires," Fire Research Note No. 953, British Joint Fire Research Organization, London, November 1972.

[20] Homans, George C., *The Human Group,* Harcourt, Brace and World, Inc., New York, 1950, pp. 11, 12, and 124.

[21] Boot and Cox, *Statistical Analysis for Managerial Decisions,* 2nd Ed., McGraw-Hill Book Company, New York, 1974, Chapter 11.

[22] Homans, George C., *The Human Group,* Chapter 16.

[23] NFPA 901 *Uniform Coding for Fire Protection,* National Fire Protection Association, Boston, 1976.

---

*The document by Richard G. Bright was prepared prior to the development of certain information regarding building details. Specifically, the door from the main north-south corridor that led to the east-west corridor (south of the Cabaret Room) was determined to be a substantial wood-panel door that was normally in the closed position. The door reportedly was equipped with spring-loaded hinges. Evidence developed from the interview transcripts indicates that the east-west corridor south of the Cabaret Room was tenable for a longer period of time than was concluded by Mr. Bright.

BIBLIOGRAPHY

Boot and Cox, *Statistical Analysis for Managerial Decisions,* 2nd Ed., McGraw-Hill Book Company, New York, 1974.

Bright, Richard G., *Beverly Hills Supper Club Fire, Southgate, Kentucky, May 28, 1977 — An Analysis of the Development and Spread of Fire from the Room of Origin (Zebra Room) to the Cabaret Room,* U.S. Department of Commerce, National Bureau of Standards, Washington, DC, September 1, 1977.

Building Materials Directory, Underwriters Laboratories Inc., Chicago, January 1976.

Homans, George C., *The Human Group,* Harcourt, Brace and World, Inc., New York, 1950.

Investigative Report To The Governor — Beverly Hills Supper Club Fire, May 28, 1977, Commonwealth of Kentucky, Frankfort, Kentucky, September 16, 1977.

NFPA 13, *Standard for the Installation of Sprinkler Systems,* National Fire Protection Association, Boston, 1976.

NFPA 70, *National Electrical Code,* National Fire Protection Association, Boston, 1975.

NFPA 101, *Code for Safety to Life from Fire in Building and Structures,* National Fire Protection Association, Boston, 1976.

NFPA 901, *Uniform Coding for Fire Protection,* National Fire Protection Association, Boston, 1976.

Officer's Handbook for Determining Cause and Circumstances of Fire, NFPA FIFI-4, National Fire Protection Association, Boston, 1974.

Schultz, D. P., *An Experimental Approach to Panic Behavior,* Office of Naval Research, Department of the Navy, Arlington, VA, 1966.

The National Building Code, American Insurance Association, New York, 1976.

Wood, P.G., "The Behavior of People in Fires," Fire Research Note No. 953, British Joint Fire Research Organization, London, November 1972.

Appendix A

QUESTIONNAIRE FORM *

BEVERLY HILLS SUPPER CLUB

Please answer the following questions by circling the number(s) corresponding to your answer.

1. Including yourself, how many people were with you when you arrived at the Supper Club?

    1. I arrived alone
    2. One other person
    3. Two other people
    4. Three other people
    5. Four other people
    6. Five other people
    7. More than five people

2. If you arrived at the Supper Club alone, go to Question #3. If you were with one or more persons, indicate who they were:

    1. Spouse
    2. Friend
    3. Relative
    4. Spouse & friend
    5. Spouse & relative
    6. Friend & relative

3. In what capacity were you attending the Supper Club?

    1. Patron
    2. Staff
    3. Fire fighter
    4. Other

4. If staff, please indicate your job title:

5. What room were you in when you became aware of a fire situation in the building?

    1. Cabaret Room
    2. Empire Room
    3. Viennese Rooms
    4. Garden Rooms
    5. Main Dining Room
    6. Main Bar
    7. Crystal Rooms
    8. Basement
    9. Other

6. How did you first become aware of a fire situation in the building?*

    1. Another patron mentioned it
    2. An employee mentioned it
    3. I noticed unusual heat
    4. I saw fire
    5. I saw smoke
    6. I smelled smoke
    7. Other, please specify:

7. How serious did you believe the fire to be after first becoming aware?*

    1. Not at all serious
    2. Only slightly serious
    3. Moderately serious
    4. Extremely serious

---

*Questions that are followed by an asterisk have been summarized into tables in Appendix B, "Summary of Questionnaire Data."

THE BEVERLY HILLS SUPPER CLUB FIRE

8. Approximately what time was it when you first observed smoke?*

   1. Prior to 7:45 P.M.
   2. 7:45 P.M.
   3. 8:00 P.M.
   4. 8:15 P.M.
   5. 8:20 P.M.
   6. 8:25 P.M.
   7. 8:30 P.M.
   8. 8:35 P.M.
   9. 8:40 P.M.
   10. 8:45 P.M.
   11. 8:50 P.M.
   12. 8:55 P.M.
   13. 9:00 P.M.
   14. 9:05 P.M.
   15. 9:10 P.M.
   16. 9:15 P.M.
   17. 9:20 P.M.
   18. Did not observe smoke

9. How sure are you of the exact time that you first observed smoke?

   1. Absolutely sure
   2. Sure within two or three minutes
   3. Sure within four or five minutes
   4. Sure within ten minutes
   5. Sure within fifteen minutes
   6. Sure within thirty minutes
   7. Not at all sure
   8. Did not observe smoke

10. Approximately what time was it when you first observed fire?*

    1. 8:30 P.M.
    2. 8:35 P.M.
    3. 8:40 P.M.
    4. 8:45 P.M.
    5. 8:50 P.M.
    6. 8:55 P.M.
    7. 9:00 P.M.
    8. 9:05 P.M.
    9. 9:10 P.M.
    10. 9:15 P.M.
    11. 9:20 P.M.
    12. Did not observe fire

11. How sure are you of the exact time when you first observed fire?

    1. Absolutely sure
    2. Sure within two or three minutes
    3. Sure within four or five minutes
    4. Sure within ten minutes
    5. Sure within fifteen minutes
    6. Sure within thirty minutes
    7. Not at all sure
    8. Did not observe fire

12. Did you notice any of the conditions below in the room you were in?*
    (Please circle as many as appropriate.)

    1. Seating in the aisles
    2. People standing because of no available seating
    3. Tables too close together
    4. Too many chairs per table
    5. I did not notice any of the above conditions
    6. Other (Please specify)

13. Were you aware of any unusual increase in room temperature before receiving notification of the fire?

    1. Yes
    2. No

14. If *YES*, do you feel that the increase in room temperature could have been due to such factors as poor air conditioning, lack of adequate ventilators, or accumulated body heat?

    1. Yes
    2. No

15. If *NO*, do you think the unusual increase could have been due to factors related to the fire?

    1. Yes
    2. No

    If NO, please indicate why not:

RECONSTRUCTION OF A TRAGEDY

16. How long after you received notice was it before you actually observed fire or smoke?*

    1. Less than one minute
    2. Within two minutes
    3. Within three minutes
    4. Within five minutes
    5. Within seven minutes
    6. Within ten minutes
    7. Within fifteen minutes
    8. Within twenty minutes
    9. Did not observe fire or smoke

17. Circle the number of any or all of the conditions listed below of which you observed:*

    1. Lights dimmed or flickered
    2. Lights went out
    3. Smoke coming from light or electrical fixtures
    4. Smoke coming from air conditioning or ventilating openings
    5. Odors
    6. None of the above observed

18. What specific actions taken by a Supper Club employee directly effected your exiting the room and building?* (Please circle one or more.)

    1. Employee told me what exit to use
    2. Employee led me out of the room
    3. Employee led me out of the building
    4. Employee unlocked the door
    5. None of the above

19. Did you have difficulty in locating an exit?*

    1. Yes
    2. No

    For either Yes or No, please comment:

20. If you had difficulty in escaping, please circle the numbered reasons below that apply:*

    1. Locked doors
    2. Confusing employee instructions
    3. Invalid employee instructions
    4. No employee instructions
    5. Access to exits blocked by people
    6. Aisles blocked by tables and chairs
    7. Poor visibility due to heavy smoke
    8. Poorly identified exit signs
    9. Inadequate lighting
    10. Does not apply
    11. Other (Please specify):

21. Upon exiting the building, did you see fire trucks on the scene?

    1. Yes
    2. No

    If Yes, specify where it was:

22. Please add below any further comments that may aid in our investigation.

Appendix B

SUMMARY OF QUESTIONNAIRE DATA

Table A.1 Question 6:
How did you first become aware of a fire situation in the building?

	All respondents	Cabaret Room	Garden Rooms	Empire Room	Main dining room	Main bar	Viennese Rooms	Crystal Rooms
Number of people responding	1094	528	104	175	53	50	45	65
1. Another patron mentioned it	9%	0%	3%	22%	15%	8%	9%	37%
2. An employee mentioned it	78%	96%	97%	60%	64%	58%	91%	8%
3. I noticed unusual heat	1%	0%	0%	2%	0%	0%	0%	12%
4. I saw fire	0%	0%	0%	0%	0%	0%	0%	0%
5. I saw smoke	5%	0%	0%	2%	15%	22%	0%	38%
6. I smelled smoke	1%	0%	0%	1%	0%	8%	0%	5%
7. Other	6%	4%	0%	14%	6%	4%	0%	0%

Table A.2 Question 7:
How serious did you believe the fire to be after first becoming aware?

	All respondents	Cabaret Room	Garden Rooms	Empire Room	Main dining room	Main bar	Viennese Rooms	Crystal Rooms
Number of people responding	1097	531	104	184	52	48	43	65
1. Not at all serious	38%	32%	65%	34%	23%	46%	40%	40%
2. Only slightly serious	35%	36%	24%	39%	54%	40%	30%	34%
3. Moderately serious	18%	23%	3%	18%	19%	8%	28%	14%
4. Extremely serious	9%	8%	8%	10%	4%	6%	2%	12%

Table A.3 Question 8:
Approximately what time was it when you first observed smoke?

	All respondents	Cabaret Room	Garden Rooms	Empire Room	Main dining room	Main bar	Viennese Rooms	Crystal Rooms
Number of people responding	975	445	99	170	52	48	35	61
1. Prior to 7:45 p.m.	0%	0%	0%	0%	0%	0%	0%	2%
2. 7:45 p.m.	1%	1%	0%	1%	0%	2%	0%	0%
3. 8:00 p.m.	0%	0%	0%	1%	0%	0%	0%	2%
4. 8:15 p.m.	0%	0%	0%	0%	0%	0%	0%	3%
5. 8:20 p.m.	0%	0%	0%	0%	0%	0%	0%	2%
6. 8:25 p.m.	1%	0%	0%	1%	0%	0%	0%	3%
7. 8:30 p.m.	1%	1%	1%	1%	0%	0%	6%	8%
8. 8:35 p.m.	1%	0%	0%	1%	0%	0%	0%	8%
9. 8:40 p.m.	3%	2%	2%	5%	4%	0%	6%	7%
10. 8:45 p.m.	6%	6%	6%	6%	4%	8%	0%	8%
11. 8:50 p.m.	8%	7%	7%	9%	17%	0%	11%	20%
12. 8:55 p.m.	12%	12%	13%	12%	8%	17%	26%	11%
13. 9:00 p.m.	19%	19%	18%	22%	15%	23%	20%	13%
14. 9:05 p.m.	20%	17%	31%	21%	31%	27%	20%	7%
15. 9:10 p.m.	16%	21%	13%	9%	12%	10%	11%	3%
16. 9:15 p.m.	9%	11%	4%	8%	6%	13%	0%	0%
17. 9:20 p.m.	3%	3%	4%	4%	4%	0%	0%	3%
18. Other	0%	0%	0%	0%	0%	0%	0%	0%

Table A.4 Question 10:
Approximately what time was it when you first observed fire?

	All respondents	Cabaret Room	Garden Rooms	Empire Room	Main dining room	Main bar	Viennese Rooms	Crystal Rooms
Number of people responding	1017	490	100	169	53	43	37	56
1. 8:30 p.m.	1%	1%	0%	2%	0%	2%	5%	7%
2. 8:35 p.m.	1%	0%	1%	1%	0%	0%	0%	9%
3. 8:40 p.m.	1%	1%	0%	1%	0%	0%	0%	4%
4. 8:45 p.m.	1%	1%	0%	3%	0%	0%	0%	0%
5. 8:50 p.m.	2%	4%	2%	0%	2%	0%	0%	4%
6. 8:55 p.m.	5%	7%	4%	0%	0%	5%	5%	13%
7. 9:00 p.m.	10%	10%	14%	9%	6%	2%	14%	13%
8. 9:05 p.m.	16%	19%	27%	10%	8%	9%	5%	13%
9. 9:10 p.m.	16%	14%	22%	20%	17%	5%	16%	13%
10. 9:15 p.m.	17%	18%	17%	20%	17%	16%	11%	4%
11. 9:20 p.m.	18%	14%	9%	22%	23%	42%	14%	14%
12. Did not observe fire	13%	12%	4%	12%	28%	19%	30%	9%

Table A.5 Question 12:
Did you notice any of the conditions below in the room you were in?

	All respondents	Cabaret Room	Garden Rooms	Empire Room	Main dining room	Main bar	Viennese Rooms	Crystal Rooms
Number of people responding	1117	536	104	188	54	50	45	65
1. Seating in the aisles	39%	77%	3%	2%	0%	2%	0%	5%
2. People standing because of no available seating	16%	25%	1%	1%	0%	38%	4%	8%
3. Tables too close together	45%	86%	4%	6%	11%	4%	0%	11%
4. Too many chairs	37%	71%	2%	4%	0%	8%	0%	23%
5. I did not notice any of the above conditions	40%	5%	88%	87%	87%	42%	82%	62%
6. Other	8%	4%	4%	3%	4%	8%	4%	15%

Table A.6 Question 16:
How long after you received notice was it before you actually observed fire or smoke?

	All respondents	Cabaret Room	Garden Rooms	Empire Room	Main dining room	Main bar	Viennese Rooms	Crystal Rooms
Number of people responding	1050	518	104	183	47	38	45	42
1. Less than one minute	26%	8%	0%	49%	72%	71%	62%	64%
2. Within two minutes	21%	26%	15%	23%	13%	5%	24%	5%
3. Within three minutes	19%	26%	24%	9%	0%	5%	9%	5%
4. Within five minutes	21%	27%	41%	9%	0%	5%	0%	12%
5. Within seven minutes	3%	3%	4%	2%	0%	8%	4%	2%
6. Within ten minutes	4%	2%	12%	3%	6%	0%	0%	10%
7. Within fifteen minutes	1%	1%	3%	2%	4%	0%	0%	2%
8. Within twenty minutes	1%	0%	1%	3%	0%	5%	0%	0%
9. Did not observe fire or smoke	3%	5%	0%	0%	4%	0%	0%	0%

Table A.7 Question 17:
Which of these conditions did you observe?

	All respondents	Cabaret Room	Garden Rooms	Empire Room	Main dining room	Main bar	Viennese Rooms	Crystal Rooms
Number of people responding	1117	536	104	188	54	50	45	65
1. Lights dimmed or flickered	15%	13%	9%	12%	20%	2%	9%	40%
2. Lights went out	19%	24%	5%	15%	19%	2%	16%	45%
3. Smoke coming from light or electrical fixtures	8%	9%	0%	5%	4%	6%	4%	14%
4. Smoke coming from A/C or ventilating openings	20%	20%	6%	19%	26%	38%	4%	28%
5. Odors	32%	27%	8%	42%	35%	48%	38%	72%
6. None of the above observed	43%	45%	72%	40%	31%	24%	51%	14%

Table A.8 Question 18:
What specific actions taken by a supper club employee directly effected your exiting the room and building?

	All respondents	Cabaret Room	Garden Rooms	Empire Room	Main dining room	Main bar	Viennese Rooms	Crystal Rooms
Number of people responding	1117	536	104	188	54	50	45	65
1. Employee told me what exit to use	68%	85%	70%	56%	48%	38%	56%	38%
2. Employee led me out of the room	9%	3%	13%	16%	17%	0%	22%	17%
3. Employee led me out of the building	9%	3%	14%	12%	11%	4%	16%	26%
4. Employee unlocked the door	1%	1%	8%	0%	0%	0%	0%	2%
5. None of the above	24%	13%	17%	34%	43%	48%	33%	40%

Table A.9 Question 19:
Did you have difficulty in locating an exit?

	All respondents	Cabaret Room	Garden Rooms	Empire Room	Main dining room	Main bar	Viennese Rooms	Crystal Rooms
Number of people responding	1092	527	104	185	54	48	43	61
1. Yes	12%	14%	0%	10%	6%	0%	5%	34%
2. No	88%	86%	100%	90%	94%	100%	95%	66%

Table A.10 Question 20:
What difficulty was encountered in escaping?

	All respondents	Cabaret Room	Garden Rooms	Empire Room	Main dining room	Main bar	Viennese Rooms	Crystal Rooms
Number of people responding	1117	536	104	188	54	50	45	65
1. Locked doors	2%	1%	2%	1%	0%	0%	0%	17%
2. Confusing employee instructions	3%	3%	0%	1%	11%	0%	0%	8%
3. Invalid employee instructions	1%	2%	0%	0%	4%	0%	0%	2%
4. No employee instructions	4%	2%	0%	5%	6%	0%	9%	9%
5. Access to exits blocked by people	21%	32%	0%	14%	4%	6%	24%	15%
6. Aisles blocked by tables and chairs	17%	35%	0%	0%	4%	0%	0%	5%
7. Poor visibility due to heavy smoke	23%	28%	0%	28%	13%	2%	20%	35%
8. Poorly identified exit signs	9%	13%	0%	2%	0%	0%	9%	20%
9. Inadequate lighting	11%	16%	0%	8%	4%	2%	4%	18%
10. Does not apply	22%	18%	33%	29%	24%	38%	9%	18%
11. Other	3%	3%	4%	3%	6%	0%	0%	8%

Appendix C

RICHARD BRIGHT'S ANALYSIS

BEVERLY HILLS SUPPER CLUB FIRE

SOUTHGATE, KENTUCKY

MAY 28, 1977

AN ANALYSIS OF THE DEVELOPMENT AND SPREAD
OF FIRE FROM THE ROOM OF FIRE ORIGIN (ZEBRA
ROOM) TO THE CABARET ROOM

Prepared by

Richard G. Bright
Senior Research Engineer
Center for Fire Research
National Bureau of Standards
Washington, D.C. 20234

September 1, 1977

Table of Contents

	Page
INTRODUCTION	1
CONSTRUCTION DETAILS PERTINENT TO THIS ANALYSIS	2
ORIGIN AND CAUSE OF THE FIRE	4
EFFECTS OF THE MAIN CORRIDOR FIRE ON THE CROSS CORRIDOR AND CABARET ROOM EXITS	6
EFFECTS OF SMOKE	7
EFFECTS OF AIR CONDITIONING	7
RAPIDITY OF SPREAD OF FIRE IN THE MAIN CORRIDOR	8
EFFECT OF NONCOMBUSTIBLE-SURFACED WALLS ON THE SPREAD OF FIRE IN THE MAIN CORRIDOR	9
CONCLUSIONS	11
FIGURE 1. Floor Plan of Beverly Hills Supper Club	12

APPENDICES

A.	DESCRIPTION OF MATERIAL SAMPLES SUBMITTED TO NBS BY STATE OF KENTUCKY	13
B.	RESULTS OF TESTS CONDUCTED ON MATERIAL SAMPLES SUBMITTED TO NBS BY STATE OF KENTUCKY	16
C.	RESULTS OF ANALYSIS OF SEAT COMPONENTS FROM GOLD-COLORED CHAIRS	18

BEVERLY HILLS SUPPER CLUB FIRE
MAY 28, 1977, SOUTHGATE, KENTUCKY

AN ANALYSIS OF THE DEVELOPMENT AND SPREAD
OF FIRE FROM THE ROOM OF ORIGIN (ZEBRA ROOM)
TO THE CABARET ROOM

Prepared By: R. G. Bright, Senior Research Engineer, Center for Fire Research, National Bureau of Standards, Washington, D.C.

Date Prepared: September 1, 1977

INTRODUCTION

Around 8:45 p.m. in the evening of May 28, 1977, a fire occurred in the Beverly Hills Supper Club located in Southgate, Kentucky. In addition to the total destruction of the Club, the fire resulted in the death of 164 persons (as of July 10, 1977). Based on on-site investigations and analyses of taped interviews with employees of the Club, it has been established[1] that the fire originated in a small, L-shaped, public room known as the Zebra Room. This room was located against the front (south)[2] wall, to the east of the main entrance.

Most of the victims of the fire were occupants of the Cabaret Room, which was located at the opposite end of the building from the Zebra Room, some 150 feet or so distant and on the same side (east) of the Club. An interior corridor, running most of the length of the Club in the east half, was a conduit in funneling the smoke, heat and fire from the Zebra Room to the Cabaret Room. Based on newspaper accounts, the Club contained somewhere in excess of 3,000 persons. Nearly all of the occupants of the spaces and rooms between the Zebra Room and the Cabaret Room were able to exit the building safely.

---

(1) See statement by the Kentucky State Fire Marshal on page 4.

(2) Although the Club did not have a true north-south, east-west orientation, such an orientation has been assumed for ease of description. See Figure No. 1 for this assumed orientation.

The purpose of this report is to provide the most likely explanation of the role of the corridor on the rapidity of spread of smoke, gases heat and flames from the Zebra Room to the Cabaret Room. What follows is based on an on-site investigation by the writer, laboratory analysis of key materials, and utilization of available scientific, fire research information.

CONSTRUCTION DETAILS PERTINENT TO THIS ANALYSIS

The pertinent construction details of the Zebra Room are described later on in this analysis under "ORIGIN AND CAUSE OF FIRE" and therefore will not be described here. The Zebra Room had two sets of double doors of wood construction, both swinging into the room. (See figure no. 1.) One set was to the west, opening into the reservationist's alcove. This west opening allowed the fire to pass into the main bar area but at some later stage in the fire sequence as these doors were in the closed position in the early stages of the fire according to the reservationist. The other doorway, to the north, opened into a small, east-west corridor, approximately 32 feet long and 20 feet wide. This small corridor opened into the main bar on the west and into the main, north-south corridor (to the Cabaret Room) on the east through a fifteen-foot wide opening. A curved, steel stairway to the second floor was located in this small corridor, just to the left (west) of the Zebra Room's north doors and against the north wall of the Zebra Room.

The ceiling of this small corridor was of concealed, kerf and spline, mineral-type, acoustical tile. Due to its mineral nature, this tile is likely to have had a very low flame spread index[3] and can be considered to be noncombustible. The walls of this small corridor were covered with a decoratively-finished, plywood paneling, somewhere between 3/16-inch and 1/4-inch in thickness, applied over wood furring strips[4]. This plywood was combustible and, although samples were not available to establish a flame spread index it was probably between 100 and 200 based on ASTM E-84

---

[3] For explanation of flame spread index see the Handbook of Fire Protection, 14th Edition, page 6-46, published by the National Fire Protection Association, 1976.

[4] The small pieces of paneling remaining in this corridor were swollen and/or delaminated making accurate measurements difficult.

testing procedures[5-6] and our knowledge of the behavior of these materials.

The floor of the small corridor was covered by a carpet installed over an underlayment (padding). The carpet was the same as used in the Zebra Room, according to the Kentucky State Crime Laboratory. Analysis of the Zebra Room carpet by the National Bureau of Standards (NBS) (Appendix A) indicates it was a nylon carpet with a low pile height (0.375 inches) and dense construction (58 oz/yd^2). The padding has not been identified but probably was of heavy, commercial grade, as this was characteristic of underlayments recovered from other portions of the Club.

The main, north-south corridor, leading north from the 15-foot wide opening within the east portion of the Club to the Cabaret Room, was approximately 8-feet wide and about 150-feet long. (See figure 1.) In addition to serving doorways to the Viennese Room on the east and the Empire Room on the west, this corridor connected to two cross corridors, one to the east along the south wall of the Cabaret Room, and one to the west between the Garden Room and the employees crossover, service corridor. This main corridor terminated outside of the principal entrance to the Cabaret Room. The cross corridor, along the south wall of the Cabaret Room, is important because of its effects on the exit of the occupants from the Cabaret Room, as will be discussed later in this analysis.

The main corridor's ceiling was of concealed, kerf and spline, mineral-type, acoustical tile, again, essentially noncombustible in nature. The floor was covered with a carpet applied over an underlayment. Based on NBS analysis (Appendix A), the carpet was essentially of woven, wool construction with a small amount (less than 10%) of acrylic fibers blended in. The pile height was 0.25 inches and weight was 78 oz/yd^2. The underlayment was identified by NBS to be jute with a pad height of 0.5 inches and a weight of 51 oz/yd^2.

---

(5) Standard Method of Test for Surface Burning Characteristics of Building Materials, ASTM E-84-70, American Society for Testing and Materials.

(6) See the Underwriters Laboratories Building Materials Directory, January 1976, page 204, for representative flame spread indices of similar materials.

The corridor walls were covered with a decoratively-finished, hardboard paneling applied over wood furring strips. This paneling was combustible and, although its flame spread index could not be determined, our experience indicates that it probably ranged somewhere between 150 and 200[7]. This paneling was applied to both walls of the corridor for its full length except for the curvilinear wall, at the west cross corridor, which was of exposed brick.

ORIGIN AND CAUSE OF THE FIRE

On June 10, 1977, a statement was presented to the press by Mr. Warren Southworth, State Fire Marshal of Kentucky. This statement contained information as to origin and cause of the fire. This information was based on reports and data collected by the fire investigation team. The statement read as follows:

> "Based on the investigation to date, including both interview evidence and evaluation and examination of physical evidence, the investigative team has concluded that the fire originated in a concealed space within the Zebra Room.
>
> "The most probable cause of ignition within this area was electrical in nature and would have been fed by combustibles located there. Specifically, the presence of concealed, combustible ceiling tile and wood materials used for supports provided a fuel supply for continued spread of the fire through the original and other concealed spaces. On-site analysis of the construction of the concealed spaces within the Zebra Room indicates that the fire burned for a considerable time prior to discovery. Interviews with occupants of the Zebra Room and adjacent areas support this conclusion.
>
> "The above-mentioned ignition sequence led to an intense heat buildup within the concealed space which ultimately resulted in the accumulation of smoke and hot gases within the Zebra Room itself. It was at this point when the fire was discovered, and attempts were made to extinguish it. Some time thereafter, various actions were initiated to notify occupants of the building and the fire department.

---

[7] See the Underwriters Laboratories, Inc., Building Materials Directory, January 1976, page 174, for representative flame spread indices of similar materials.

> "During the time attempts were being made to extinguish the fire within the Zebra Room, flash-over occurred. In other words, simultaneous ignition of all combustible materials within the room occurred.
>
> "Following the occurrence of flash-over, the fire continued to build until it broke out of the Zebra Room through double doors located at the north end of the room. The fire then spread rapidly throughout the structure."

When flash-over occurred in the Zebra Room, the room resembled a furnace in that all of the combustible furnishings in the room were burning simultaneously. These furnishings included several wood tables, about 20 or more chairs (see Appendix C for details on the chairs), and the carpet. Under these circumstances the walls of the rooms, which were covered with 3/16-inch, combustible hardboard paneling applied over wood furring strips, would also have been burning and contributing to the fire. What follows is a most probable scenario for the action of the fire.

This furnace-like fire had only one immediate flue or vent available to it and this was the pair of doors at the north end of the room. From eye-witness accounts, apparently one door, the west leaf, was partially open, perhaps at 45 degrees or so (confirmed by on-site evidence). It was likely the other leaf was open also, and the physical evidence suggested that it may have been fully open. Regardless of whether this leaf was open, partially open, or closed, this would have been of significance only through the first minutes of the fire as the fire's intensity was of such magnitude that the fire would have quickly consumed the top part of this wooden door.

The venting of the fire through this doorway resulted in the passage of smoke, flames and heat through the upper part of the doorway at relatively high velocities, with an inrush of cold, fresh air, at lower velocities, near the floor. As the smoke, flames and hot gases left the Zebra Room they were propelled across the ceiling of the small corridor directly outside the Zebra Room until they hit the far wall, some 20 feet distant. Here, the flames and hot gases split, with part of flames and hot gases turning down and part turning sideways in both direction. The thin, plywood paneling, on the far wall of the small corridor, would have ignited readily under the impact of this flame and hot gas exposure.

5

In the meantime, the fire on the carpet in the Zebra Room would have spread through the doorway also, slower than the flames and hot gases along the ceiling, but sustained by the thermal radiation down onto the carpet by the smoke and hot gas layer at the ceiling. In examination of the Zebra Room, it was found that the carpet and its padding were completely consumed, down to bare concrete, in the doorway opening, the only location in the Zebra Room with such extensive damage.

The flames and hot gases leaving the Zebra Room, in addition to impinging on the plywood paneling of the small corridor wall, also were probably passing up the stairway to the west of the lobby, into the main bar to the west, and through the 15-foot opening into the main corridor to the east.

It was apparent, from the on-site investigation, that sufficient heat was present in the stream of hot gases passing through this 15-foot opening into the main corridor to ignite combustibles present in this corridor. These combustibles consisted of the hardboard paneling on the walls and the carpet system on the floor.

As the flames and hot gases entered the main corridor, the carpet and the hardboard paneling began to contribute combustible gases to the fire through the driving off of the combustible volatiles in the carpet and the paneling. This resulted in the extension of the burning down the corridor. At about this period in time, sufficient thermal radiation was being directed down on the carpet surface from the smoke and hot gas layer at the ceiling to cause the spread of the fire on the carpet from the small corridor through the 15-foot doorway, into the main corridor. Once this happened, the fire in the corridor was very nearly a self-sustaining fire, feeding on both the carpet and the paneling, with each contributing to the growth and spread of the other. Even so, energy was still being supplied into the main corridor from the fire in the Zebra Room and the small corridor outside. From this point, fire spread rapidly down the main corridor, with visible fire rolling along underneath the ceiling and a secondary fire traveling along on the carpet face, trailing behind the ceiling fire.

EFFECTS OF THE MAIN CORRIDOR FIRE ON THE CROSS CORRIDOR AND CABARET ROOM EXITS

When the main corridor fire reached the first cross corridor, the corridor behind the south wall of the Cabaret Room, the fire extended down this cross corridor as well as down the main corridor. If this scenario is correct then this had an unfortunate consequence for those occupants still in the Cabaret Room as one of the secondary exits for the Cabaret Room was across this corridor to a door leading to the outside of the building. (See figure 1.) In other words, as fire came down this cross corridor, it cut-off this exit from usage by the Cabaret Room occupants. At the same time, the fire in the main corridor was in the process of closing off the main entrance door to the Cabaret Room. So, in effect, the main corridor fire blocked two of the three exits available to the Cabaret Room occupants leaving them with only the exit in the northeast corner of the room which passed through the service bar area. Shortly after the fire in the main and cross corridor rendered these exits unsafe for use, the fire began to penetrate the Cabaret Room through these very same exit doors.

EFFECTS OF SMOKE

The effects of smoke on the Club's occupants has been deliberately omitted from the above analysis. Based on our experience with corridor fires, the smoke from the original fire in the Zebra Room and from the fire in the corridors would have spread in the same direction as the fire, but at an earlier period in this sequence. In other words, the smoke would have reached the Cabaret Room some time ahead of the fire. This smoke would have appeared to be dark, almost black in nature, to the occupants. In addition, it would have been extremely irritating, causing tearing of the eyes and a burning sensation to the nose. This was due to the nature of the materials undergoing combustion, i.e., the carpets and wall paneling. In addition, for a fire of this type, the smoke would have contained certain toxic gas species, the principal one being carbon monoxide. Carbon monoxide, although colorless and odorless in the quantities likely to have been present in the early stages of this fire, produces confusion and disorientation. Later, of course, as the levels increased, carbon monoxide produced unconsciousness and ultimately death among some of the occupants.

EFFECTS OF AIR CONDITIONING

The public spaces of the Supper Club were completely air conditioned and it was in operation at the time of the fire. There was no central system but rather a series of separate systems serving various areas. It is not clear whether the air conditioning systems had any adverse effects, such as spreading or retarding the movement of smoke or of the fire, at least during the early stages of the fire. What is clear, however, is that once the fire left the Zebra Room, the fire was probably of sufficient energy to overpower the air handling system. It was suggested, in some newspaper accounts, that the air conditioning system helped spread the smoke and the fire. This hypothesis may or may not be true but the smoke and the fire would have had no difficulty spreading throughout the Club and through the public use spaces, such as the corridors, as there were no barriers to the movement of smoke and fire through these spaces and the fire had sufficient thermal energy to move the smoke through these spaces.

RAPIDITY OF SPREAD OF FIRE IN THE MAIN CORRIDOR

The rapidity of the spread of fire from the Zebra Room to the Cabaret Room, via the main corridor, undoubtedly was a factor in the large loss of life in the Cabaret Room. While it is not possible to give more than an educated estimate, from the experience of this writer, it is postulated that once the fire had emerged from the Zebra Room and crossed over into the main corridor, the fire probably reached the Cabaret Room in somewhere between two and five minutes. Some of the Viennese Room patrons were ushered out of the Viennese Room by employees, across the main corridor, through the Empire Room, through the kitchen and out. One of the members of this party has reported that he looked back as they were crossing the Empire Room and could see fire in the main corridor. These patrons were probably ushered out of the Viennese Room some two to three minutes after flash-over had occurred in the Zebra Room.

Research activities here at NBS on full-scale corridor fire experiments have indicated that the rapid spread of fires may be possible in corridors when the only combustible present in the corridor are some types of carpet/underlayment combinations[8-10]. If there is a movement of air in the

---

(8) Fung, F., Et al, The NBS Program on Corridor Fires, Fire Journal, Vol. 67, No. 3, pp 41-48, May 1973.

(9) Quintere, J.G., A Charaterization and Analysis of NBS Corridor Fire Experiments in Order to Evaluate the Behavior and Performance of Floor Covering Materials, Nat. Bur. of Stds., NBSIR 75-691, June 1975.

(10) Alderson, S., Et al, Evaluation of the Fire Performance of Carpet Underlayments, Nat. Bur. of Stds., NBSIR 76-1018, Sept. 1976.

corridor in the direction of the fire spread, this air movement may increase the rapidity of fire spread, once the fire has entered the corridor.

Research conducted at IIT Research Institute[11] has shown that a fire can spread down a corridor when the corridor has noncombustible floors and ceilings but the walls are covered with continuous, floor-to-ceiling, combustible paneling with flame spread indices in excess of 59. The main corridor in the Beverly Hills Supper Club not only had a combustible carpet assembly on the floor but also had wall linings with a flame spread index of somewhere between 100 and 200. There was probably some air movement in the corridor, but the precise nature, quantity, speed, and direction are unknown.

Our experience with simulated corridor fire tests would indicate that this configuration of materials and geometry will produce a rapid spread of fire down a corridor such as this one.

EFFECT OF NONCOMBUSTIBLE-SURFACED WALLS ON THE SPREAD OF FIRE IN THE MAIN CORRIDOR

The carpet/underlayment system used in the main corridor of the Club was subjected to the NBS-developed flooring radiant panel. (See Appendix B.) This panel, which is described elsewhere[12], essentially measures the amount of thermal radiant energy necessary to cause a fire to spread on a flooring system. Many carpets, and the one used in the main corridor is an example, will not propagate fire from a simple ignition source, such as a dropped cigarette or match. However, if the carpet is preheated at an increasing rate, such as by a thermal radiation from a smoke and hot gas layer at the ceiling, a point is reached where the heating and generation of hot gases is sufficient for the ignition of the carpet from a small, external flame. If the heating continues, the fire will spread along the carpet indefinitely, as long as the thermal radiation from the ceiling hot gas layer continues. The flooring radiant panel permits a determination to be made as to how much thermal energy is necessary to promote fire spread along the carpet face. The results are given in terms of critical radiant flux.

---

(11) Waterman, T. E., Corridor Flame Spread, Fire Journal, Vol. 67, No. 6, pp 66-72, Nov. 1973.

(12) Benjamin, I.A., Et al, The Flooring Radiant Panel Test and Proposed Criteria, Fire Journal, Vol. 70, No. 2, pp 63-70, March 1976.

As stated above, the carpet/underlayment assembly from the main corridor was tested by NBS in the flooring radiant panel. The critical radiant flux was found to be an average of 0.78 watts per square centimeter. What this means is that the carpet assembly had relatively good resistance to the propagation of flame under thermal radiation exposure as compared to other commercially-available carpets. (The higher the number, the better.) Table I gives results of several carpet assemblies (with underlayment) tested in NBS' flooring radiant panel. As can be seen from this comparison, the main corridor carpet assembly was better than any of these in terms of resistance to propagation of flame under thermal radiation exposure. However, if the thermal radiation exceeds the critical radiant flux, then a fire can be expected to spread along the carpet face.

TABLE 1

Flooring Radiant Panel Results - Carpet with Underlayment
(Typical Values)

Type of Material	Critical Radiant Flux
*Wool and Hair Jute	0.66
*Acrylic and Hair Jute	0.25
*Nylon A and Hair Jute	< 0.10
*Nylon B and Hair Jute	0.35
*Polyester A and Hair Jute	< 0.10
*Polyester B and Hair Jute	< 0.10
Beverly Hills-Wool and Jute	0.78

*Alderson, S. and Breden, L., Evaluation of the Fire Performance of Carpet Underlayments, Nat. Bur. of Stds., NBSIR 76-1018, Sept. 1976.

In the writer's opinion, the main contributor to the continued and extensive build up of thermal radiation in the main corridor, sufficient to promote the continued burning of carpet, was probably the combustible wall paneling.

It appears that if the walls of the main corridor had been covered with a noncombustible material, in lieu of the hardboard paneling used, and the same carpet assembly was in place as was actually used, there may not have been a rapid, extensive spread of fire along this corridor.

CONCLUSIONS

1. Once the Zebra Room was fully involved in fire, i.e., flashover had occurred, sufficient thermal energy was available to push the fire out of the north, double doors into the small corridor outside.

2. Sufficient thermal energy was available from the Zebra Room to ignite and sustain a fire in this small corridor on the carpet and plywood wall paneling.

3. The combination of the thermal energy outputs of the Zebra Room and small corridor were of sufficient magnitude to ignite and sustain a fire in the main corridor to the Cabaret Room.

4. Once the fire was established in the main corridor, the fire progressed rapidly towards the Cabaret Room, probably reaching the Cabaret Room some two to five minutes after entering the main corridor.

5. The fire in the main corridor also spread laterally in the small cross corridor behind the south wall of the Cabaret Room.

6. The combination of the fire in the main corridor and in the cross corridor ultimately blocked two of the three exits from the Cabaret Room leaving the remaining occupants with only one exit through the service bar area to the outside.

7. The air conditioning system does not appear to have played any significant role in the spread of fire towards the Cabaret Room.

RECONSTRUCTION OF A TRAGEDY

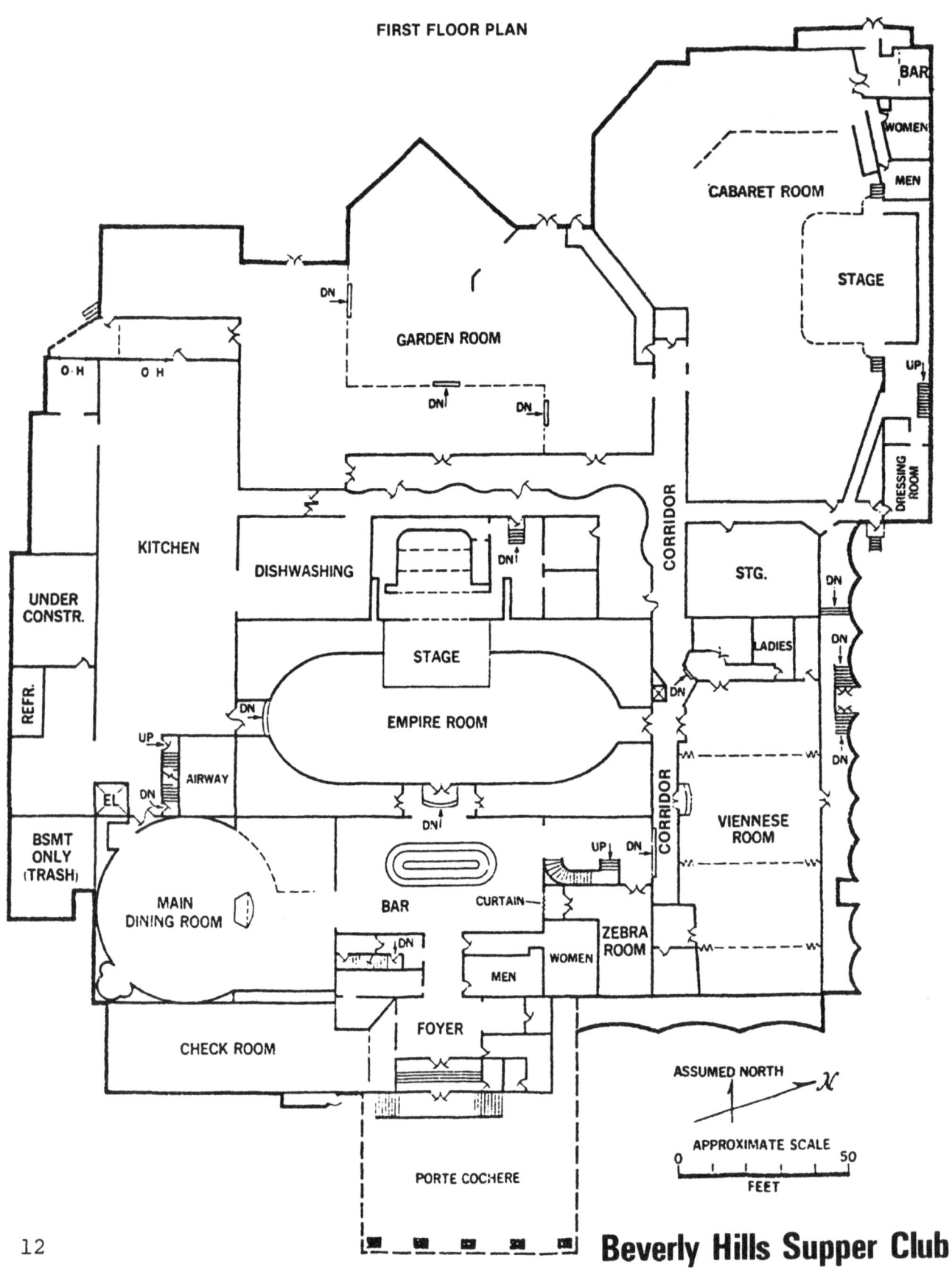

FIRST FLOOR PLAN

Beverly Hills Supper Club

APPENDIX A - DESCRIPTION OF MATERIAL SAMPLES SUBMITTED TO
             NBS BY STATE OF KENTUCKY

State Exhibit 72 and 73

   Kentucky Description - Carpet and padding from Zebra Room.

   NBS Identification - Carpet is of dense construction consisting of low loops with a cut pile. Outer pile is nylon. Carpet has netting sublayer of olefin and a backing of jute. Pile height is 0.375 inches and weight is 58 oz/yd^2.

   Padding is of waffle design of latex rubber. The pad is backed with thin polyester. Pad weight is 74 oz/yd^2.

   Remarks - No further tests were conducted on these samples, particularly the carpet, as both had been exposed to fire.

State Exhibit 78

   Kentucky Description - Sample of acoustical tile from basement storage.

   NBS Identification - Aluminum-backed, mineral-type, acoustical tile, 23-3/4" x 23-3/4" x 3/4" thick. White finish, Glacier Shadowline pattern. Manufacturer unknown. Weight was 19 lbs/ft^3. Surface pattern resembles acoustical plaster.

   Remarks - Location where used in the Club is not known. Subjected to Radiant Panel Flame Spread Test, ASTM E-162. Results in Appendix B.

State Exhibit 79

   Kentucky Description - Sample of carpet padding from Cabaret Room.

   NBS Identification - Foam rubber underlayment with thin paper backing. Height - 0.25 inches. Weight - 87 oz/yd^2.

   Remarks - No further tests conducted on this sample.

State Exhibit 80

   Kentucky Description - Sample of carpet padding taken from storage in basement of same type as used in corridor leading to Cabaret Room.

   NBS Identification - Underlayment is of jute with a height of 0.5 inches (uncompressed) and with a weight of 51 oz/yd^2.

   Remarks - This underlayment was used in conjunction with State Exhibit 81 for several tests as a carpet/underlayment assembly. See Appendix B for results of tests.

State Exhibit 81

   Kentucky Description - Sample of carpet taken from storage in basement of same type as used in corridor leading to Cabaret Room and same type as used in Cabaret Room.

   NBS Identification - Carpet is of tightly woven wool construction with a low, cut pile. The carpet has two sublayers. One is of cotton and the other is of jute. Pile height is 0.25 inches and carpet weight is 78 oz/yd^2. The carpet has been blended with another fiber believed to be nylon. The nylon appears to constitute less than 10% of the carpet face.

   Remarks - Several tests were conducted on this carpet as an assembly using the underlayment identified as State Exhibit 80. This carpet/underlayment assembly represents the actual carpet/underlayment assembly that was present on the floor of the main corridor between the Zebra Room and the Cabaret Room the night of the fire. See Appendix B for results of tests.

State Exhibit 88

   Kentucky Description - Two (2) sheets of masonite paneling from storage.

   NBS Identification - Hardboard paneling with simulated walnut decorative face. Thickness - 0.25 inches. Weight - 48 lbs/ft^3.

   Remarks - Location where used in Club, not known. Samples subjected to Radiant Panel Flame Spread Test, ASTM E-162 and to Smoke Density Chamber Test, NFPA-258, See results in Appendix B.

14

State Exhibit 90

   Kentucky Description - Ceiling tile from storage of type believed to have been in corridor to Cabaret Room.

   NBS Identification - Mineral-type, fissured surface, acoustical tile. Dimensions - 12" x 12" x 3/4". Designed for kerf and spline (concealed) installation. Approximate weight - 22 lbs/ft^3.

   Remarks - Specimens were subjected to Radiant Panel Flame Spread Test, ASTM E-162. See Appendix B for results.

APPENDIX B - RESULTS OF TESTS CONDUCTED ON MATERIAL SAMPLES
SUBMITTED TO NBS BY STATE OF KENTUCKY

Radiant Panel Flame Spread Test Results - ASTM E-162

Exhibit No.	I_s
78	35
81 & 80	322
88	129
90	19

Remarks: All results are the average of four runs except 78 and 90 which were the average of only two runs each due to sample quantity limitations. The flame spread indicies for the mineral tiles (#78 and 90), were as expected as was the flame spread index for the paneling (#88). The flame spread index for the carpet/underlayment assembly (#81 and 80) were about as to be expected considering the thickness of the assembly which was 0.75 inches.

Flooring Radiant Panel Test Results

Exhibit No.	Critical Radiant Flux W/cm^2
81 and 80	0.78

Remarks: The critical radiant flux of 0.78 W/cm^2 is the average of these runs. The performance of the carpet/underlayment was good, relative to other commercially-available carpets. This is to be expected from wool carpets which tend to resist flame spread to a higher degree than carpets of other fibers.

Smoke Density Chamber Test Results - NFPA 258

Exhibit No.	Exposure F or N	Max. Specific Optical Density (Corrected)	Indicated Gas Concentrations in PPM		
			HCl	HCN	CO
81 & 80	F	395	12	31	1000
81 & 80	N	450	-	-	-
88	F	95	0	2	1500
88	N	580	-	-	-

16

Remarks:

1. F is for flaming exposure, N is for nonflaming exposure.

2. Results are the average of three trials.

3. The toxic gas determinations were conducted on one trial only and were done by taking grab samples with Drager tube colometric indicators.

4. Results were as expected from the types of materials tested. The carpet/underlayment yielded fairly high smoke generation numbers in both the flaming and nonflaming modes. The hardboard paneling gave low numbers flaming and high numbers in nonflaming mode characteristic of a wood-based products. The major toxic gas component was carbon monoxide (CO) again characteristic of these types of materials.

UNITED STATES DEPARTMENT OF COMMERCE
National Bureau of Standards
Washington, D.C. 20234

June 16, 1977

MEMORANDUM FOR Mr. R. Bright

From: Maya Paabo & James Brown

Subject: Analysis of seat components from Kentucky fire

The seat cover and padding samples were analyzed for the basic polymer composition by infrared spectroscopy and for elements indicative of a fire retardant (e.g. Cl, Br, P and Sb) by x-ray fluorescence. The results of the analyses are listed in the attached table.

Of the five samples analyzed none appear to be fire retarded. The seat cover exhibits a high chloride content because of the presence of polyvinyl chloride. The outside back padding contains chlorine only as a minor component. Without a detectable quantity of phosphorus, this is being interpreted that no fire retardants are present.

18

Sample No.		Polymer ID	Elemental Composition Major	Minor
103-1	Seat cover	PVC*	Cl, Pb	Ca,Cr,Fe,Al,Si
103-2	Padding, inside back	Polyurethane, TDI/polyether type	—	Si,S,Sn
103-3	Padding, outside back	Polyurethane, TDI/polyether type	—	Si,S,Cl,Sn,Ca
103-4a	Padding, seat white layer	Polyurethane, TDI/polyether type	S,Ba	Sr,Sn
103-4b	Padding, seat green layer	Styrene/butadiene rubber	K,Zn	Si,S,Ca,Fe

* Plasticized with 2-ethylhexyl **decyl** phthalate and filled with calcium carbonate